Entrepreneur
MAGAZINE'S

ULTIMATE
GUIDE TO

Email Marketing
FOR BUSINESS

- Produce low-cost, high-impact email marketing campaigns
- Attract leads and turn them into customers, brand ambassadors, and revenue generators

Entrepreneur
PRESS

SUSAN GUNELIUS

Entrepreneur Press, Publisher
Cover Design: Andrew Welyczko
Production and Composition: Eliot House Productions

This publication is designed to provide accurate and authoritative information in regard to the
subject matter covered. It is sold with the understanding that the publisher is not engaged in
rendering legal, accounting or other professional services. If legal advice or other expert assistance is
required, the services of a competent professional person should be sought.

Library of Congress Cataloging-in-Publication Data
　　Names: Gunelius, Susan, author.
　　Title: Entrepreneur magazine's ultimate guide to email marketing for business / by
　　　　Susan Gunelius.
　　Other titles: Ultimate guide to email marketing for business | Entrepreneur (Santa Monica, Calif.)
　　Description: Irvine, California: Entrepreneur Media, Inc., [2018] | Includes index.
　　Identifiers: LCCN 2018001412| ISBN 978-1-59918-623-8 (alk. paper) | ISBN 1-59918-623-3
　　　　(alk. paper)
　　Subjects: LCSH: Electronic mail marketing. | Internet marketing.
　　Classification: LCC HF5415.1265 .G864 2018 | DDC 658.8/72—dc23
　　LC record available at https://lccn.loc.gov/2018001412

Printed in the United States of America

22 21 20 19 18　　　　　　　　　　　　　　　　　　　10 9 8 7 6 5 4 3 2 1

Contents

Acknowledgments

This book is dedicated to my husband, Scott, and my children, Brynn, Daniel, and Ryan, without whom I never would have started on this journey as an author and business owner. It's been a crazy ride, but I wouldn't trade a day for anything. The best is yet to come.

I'd also like to acknowledge my literary agent, Bob Diforio of D4EO Literary Agency, for his guidance and support as well as the entire team at Entrepreneur Press and Entrepreneur.com. This book would not have come to life without every person's help to get it into readers' hands.

Finally, I'd like to thank my parents for paying for my undergraduate degree in marketing, which started everything, and thank you to my former colleagues who challenged me, taught me, and gave me the tools I needed to be successful throughout my marketing career.

Foreword by Jason VandeBoom
Founder and CEO, ActiveCampaign

Even today, decades after email's invention, email marketing remains the most effective medium for reaching your customers, and it's an integral part of shaping their experience of your business. While communication continues to evolve, email remains an important part of the mix for businesses. It's a fast, effective way to send and receive asynchronous messages, both personally and professionally.

For a business like yours, it's ideal because you can make your email campaigns:

- *Targeted to your audience.* You're able to send an email to the exact group of contacts who would be most interested. Just as important, this means you're not sending that message to people who would have no interest.
- *Personalized for each individual.* Your message can be dynamically tailored so that different individuals see different message content depending on what would be most relevant to them.
- *Perfectly timed based on each person's behavior and other insight.* Email messages can be triggered to send based on any number of factors, such as making a purchase, clicking a link in a campaign, visiting a specific web page, and more. Marketing automation has taken email marketing to the next level.

These are strengths no other marketing medium offers. You can't do all this with radio or TV ads, search engine traffic, display ads, or social media platforms. Ultimately, these unique advantages are only important because they help you create a better experience for each customer at each stage of the customer lifecycle—as someone progresses from "new lead" and transforms into an "outspoken advocate."

Part of creating a better experience is learning about your contacts' needs and interests so that you can send better campaigns. A customer is going to have a better experience with your email marketing when they're receiving content and messages that are relevant and interesting to them. The great thing about these intelligence-driven campaigns is that you'll send fewer emails. When you do, counterintuitively, you'll achieve better results because you'll see better engagement and you'll have a stronger relationship with your list of customers.

Unfortunately, customer experience often takes a backburner for a focus on "what works." This is unfortunate because "what works" and "positive customer experience" work hand-in-hand, and effective marketing is the natural end product of an overwhelmingly positive customer experience. Focusing on creating the best possible customer experience simplifies decision making for you as a marketer. It's a straightforward rule of thumb that applies just as much to marketing as it does to business in general—if you do what's in the best interest of each customer, you'll end up with a growing, passionate, and outspoken customer base.

Your Power Is in Your Email Marketing List

As an entrepreneur or marketer, your success lies very much in what you can control, and one of the most valuable and powerful things you own and control is your email marketing list. The growing acceptance of permission-based email marketing has turned what was once considered a spammer's tactic into a core marketing strategy for businesses of all sizes. You can harness the power of your email marketing list to grow your business, and this book shows you exactly how to do it.

Today's consumers are inundated with messages at every moment of every day. From traditional media like TV, radio, and ambient experiences to social media, online advertising, online video, and, yes, email marketing, the amount of communication clutter people are exposed to on a daily basis continues to increase. Standing out in a crowded world—both online and offline—is more difficult than ever. Making matters worse is the constant changing of the rules, particularly in the social media and search engine optimization space where players like Facebook and Google seem to adjust their rules every day.

Successful business owners and marketers must be extremely agile and ready to adapt to those changing rules at any moment. Of course, this takes time and money, and with most forms of marketing, there is no guarantee that your efforts will be noticed or effective. But what if I told you there is a way to get your messages in front of people who want to hear from you? What if there was a way to not just get your messages in front of these people but also track how they engage with your messages, which messages drive them to action, and which messages they share with other people? Email marketing is the solution.

The *Ultimate Guide to Email Marketing for Business* introduces you to some of the ways you can use email marketing to grow your business. By focusing on building a strong foundation first, you'll learn how to develop a comprehensive email marketing program that can evolve with your business goals. From attracting subscribers to converting them into buying customers and vocal brand advocates, you'll discover the techniques that email marketing professionals use to derive positive results from permission-based marketing via email.

This book begins by introducing you to some basics that are essential to understand if you're going to truly leverage the power of email marketing. Most important, you'll learn what a "marketing funnel" is and how to create funnels that lead to conversions, which can be sales or any other type of conversion action you want your subscribers to complete. You'll also learn about the laws and deliverability rules you must follow to ensure people receive your messages, and you'll discover a variety of tools to help you along the way.

Once you understand the basics, you'll learn techniques to grow your subscriber list, such as making your opt-in form easily accessible and using free content to encourage people to subscribe. With your list actively growing through the lead generation techniques discussed in this book, you'll next learn how to develop conversion funnels that drive people to take a specific action, such as making a purchase, signing up for a webinar, or any other action you desire. In addition, you'll be introduced to list segmentation techniques so you can ensure the right people get the right messages from you at the right times. That's how you boost conversions!

When you have one or more conversion funnels in place, you'll learn how to automate some of your email marketing processes to save time and keep your subscribers engaged with your brand. Of course, an email marketing plan is only as good as the results it generates, so you'll also be introduced to some key metrics you should use to analyze performance, as well as popular methods for testing your messages and improving your results. Finally, you'll get a complete collection of resources and swipe files, which are files you can simply copy and paste to create your own campaigns and materials, so you can start immediately implementing everything you learn in this book.

If you follow the rules of email marketing, attract the right target audiences, and send those people relevant messages, your efforts will pay off in the form of increased brand awareness, word-of-mouth marketing, brand loyalty, and sales. The best part about email marketing is that it doesn't have to be expensive. By leveraging the free and affordable tools available to you today, you can develop an email marketing plan that will deliver positive results for your business. Keep reading to learn how to do it.

Chapter 1

The Evolution of Email Marketing

The email marketing of today is not the same as email marketing just five years ago. So much has changed in such a short time that it can be challenging for entrepreneurs to keep up, but staying current on the dos and don'ts of email marketing is critical for your business' success. The reason is simple. Today, the power is in your list.

Email marketing is an essential part of an integrated marketing strategy, but even if yours is a microbusiness or you're a solopreneur with an extremely small budget, email marketing should still be a priority for you. Why? Because email is where most people prefer to get news from companies and brands about promotions, discounts, and more.

Here's some context. According to Radicati's 2016 "Email Statistics" report (http://radicati.com/wp/wp-content/uploads/2016/01/Email_Statistics_Report_2016-2020_Executive_Summary.pdf), email will be used by 3 billion people in 2020, which is nearly half the world's population. Of the people who won't use email by 2020, 1.6 billion of them do not have electricity. That means, if you're selling to consumers in the developed world, the people you're trying to reach with your brand messages are using email. If you're not showing up in their email inboxes, you're missing a significant opportunity to grow your brand and business.

> The power is in your list.

THE BIRTH OF EMAIL MARKETING (AND THE CHALLENGING TEEN YEARS)

The first email message was sent in 1971, and the first mass email message was sent to 100 people in 1978. However, it wasn't until the 1990s that email use became widespread. First, the internet debuted in 1991. Five years later, the first web-based email service launched as HoTMaIL. I graduated from college in 1993 and my first job was working in the marketing department of a division of AT&T. At the time, most people in the company didn't have email, and those who did used AT&T's home-grown email solution. Within a couple of years, every employee had Microsoft Outlook and email had become a critical part of the workday. Today, it's hard to imagine life without email.

The point of the story is that it didn't take long for email to become critical to business and life. As a result, marketers discovered that connecting with consumers via email gave them yet another way to promote products and services. But a problem arose fairly quickly—spam. By the late 1990s, email marketing had grown to its awkward teenage years where it seemed out of control. As a result, lawmakers stepped in to keep consumers safe from unwanted email solicitations.

In 1998, the Data Protection Act was updated in the United Kingdom to include email opt-out. Five years later, the CAN-SPAM Act of 2003 was passed in the U.S. and privacy and electronic regulations were passed in Europe. It took another five years for Canada's Anti-Spam Law to be passed. Bottom line, the proliferation of unwanted email messages sent by companies became such a problem for consumers that countries had to pass laws to stop them. If you're sending email messages from your business, you still need to follow these laws today. Don't worry—you'll learn more about them in Chapter 3.

It was during this spam-heavy period in the late 1990s and early 2000s that email marketing got a bad reputation. Large companies with deep pockets could buy lists of consumer email addresses and send mass messages that may or may not have been relevant to recipients. Fortunately, anti-spam laws helped curb the volume of unwanted messages, so the messages that people truly *did* want to receive from companies could get to the right recipients.

EMAIL MARKETING TODAY (LOOK WHO'S ALL GROWN UP)

As we entered the late 2000s, something very big happened that would change email marketing forever. Email marketing service providers made email marketing available to the masses. The idea that email could be more than just a way to communicate between friends had been embraced within the marketing departments of large companies, but it wasn't until companies like Constant Contact, AWeber, MailChimp, iContact, VerticalResponse, and Infusionsoft developed email marketing technology as a software-as-a-service product that it started on its path to becoming a critical part of every marketing plan. *Software as a Service* (SaaS) is a software distribution model. The software provider hosts the application and makes it available to users online, rather than allowing users to install it locally on their computers.

SaaS products made email marketing affordable and easy. Thanks to 24/7 access, low monthly subscription fees, and easy-to-use tools, anyone could build email lists from their websites, create professional-looking email messages, and send those messages to groups of people at specific times. Promoting sales, sending discount codes, and announcing new products to people who had already opted in to receive these types of messages was suddenly easier than ever.

And that's where we are today. Email marketing is mature, stable, and effective. Remember, the power is in your list. You just need to learn how to build that list and use it to turn subscribers into paying customers and brand advocates. Fortunately, that's exactly what you'll learn in this book.

WHY YOU SHOULD INVEST IN EMAIL MARKETING

Just like every marketing tool that is available for you to connect your brand with consumers, email marketing has pros and cons. You should understand what you're getting into before you invest in an email marketing application. Email marketing is one of the most cost-effective investments you can make to promote your products and services, but it's not perfect.

Advantages of Email Marketing

Let's start with the pros. Email marketing has more advantages than disadvantages since consumers have become more accepting of it during the past decade. To determine if email marketing is right for you and your business, consider these advantages.

Affordability

If you or an existing member of your team can manage your email marketing programs and learn how to use your chosen email marketing application, then it's an extremely affordable way to connect with large numbers of people who have expressed interest in your products or services (since you can send email messages only to people who have opted into your list by law—see Chapter 3 for legal details).

Email marketing service providers typically offer their software at low monthly fees. They might charge you based on the number of subscribers on your list, the number of messages you send per month, or a combination of the two. For example, some providers offer plans that allow you to send messages to a small list for free or for less than $10 per month. You'll learn more about these providers and their applications in Chapter 4. For now, understand that pricing usually starts quite low and increases as you add more subscribers to your list or send a higher volume of messages.

Effectiveness

According to the Direct Marketing Association's "National Client Email Report 2015" (http://emailmonday.com/wp-content/uploads/2015/04/National-client-email-2015-DMA.pdf), for every dollar you spend on email marketing, the average return you can expect is $38. Of course, that return isn't guaranteed, but if you test, tweak, and optimize your campaigns, it's very achievable. Furthermore, Forrester's "Social Relationship Strategies That Work" report revealed that people are very willing to receive email messages from businesses. Forrester found they're twice as likely to sign up to a business' email list than they are to interact with a business on Facebook. In other words, despite all the hype that Facebook marketing gets, consumers are more engaged with email marketing. Whether you're using email marketing to drive more website traffic or increase conversions and sales, email marketing is an important piece of your marketing plan.

Measurability

Most email marketing tools give you access to a lot of data about your subscribers and their behaviors. For example, you can quickly learn who opened your email messages and clicked the links in your messages. Using this data, you can test elements of your email campaigns, such as subject lines, time of delivery, and more. When you set up email automation sequences, you can even track where people fell out of your marketing funnel and develop new ways to not just keep them in the funnel but continue moving them through it to a conversion (see Chapter 5 for more information about funnels and sequencing).

You can even integrate your email marketing tool with Google Analytics to do a deeper dive into subscribers' behaviors. The information you collect could help you create additional email campaigns as well as ad retargeting campaigns. In fact, all this data can get overwhelming, but don't worry. You'll learn all about tracking email marketing performance in Chapter 12.

Customization and Personalization

Email marketing applications make it easy for you to customize your email messages. You can change the layout, colors, images, fonts, and so on to match your brand and appeal to your audience. Many applications provide easy drag-and-drop design editors so you can create a highly professional email message quickly. In addition, tools that offer advanced sequencing, segmentation, and automation features allow you to customize every element of your email messages for your target audience.

Personalized email messages often generate higher open and click through rates. You can test personalizing the subject line of your email messages by adding the recipient's name, or you can test personalizing the greeting within the body of the message (such as "Dear Bob"). Personalization doesn't always work perfectly, but if you're confident that your list contains accurate recipient names, it could make a big difference in the success of your campaigns. It's a perfect element to test.

Segmentation

Who are you sending email messages to? Do you know where they are in your marketing funnel and what they want or need from you to continue pushing them through the funnel to conversion? An email marketing application that provides segmentation features allows you to segment by a variety of factors (depending on what information you've captured from your subscribers), such as age, geographic location, birth date, anniversary date (of when they became your customer), average order value, date of last purchase, and more. You can segment your list of subscribers and send targeted email messages to groups of people based on the criteria you choose. For example, you might set up an email automation that automatically sends a coupon to prior customers on their birthdays. This is a great way to increase loyalty.

Segmentation can increase open rates, click-throughs, and conversions. Some email marketing applications offer advanced segmentation features so you can segment by behaviors. For example, you set up a sequence that sends an email message to your list of customers that offers a special price on a product for sale on your website. Those recipients who click on the link in the email to get the offer are taken to a special landing page on your site where they can click the "buy" button and make a purchase. People who make the purchase would then be segmented separately from those who did not make a purchase. The buyers would receive a follow-up email sequence offering related products and services while the nonbuyers would receive reminders that the discount is expiring soon. You can get very complex in your segmentation and automation processes in an effort to increase conversions.

Relationship and Trust Building

One of the most important aspects of building a successful business is building a brand that consumers recognize and trust. Email marketing gives you the opportunity to demonstrate your authority on your subject matter so consumers trust that you know what you're talking about. They'll develop perceptions of your brand based on the email messages you send, and when the time comes that they're ready to make a purchase, they'll choose your brand.

This is particularly important for businesses that sell products and services where purchase decisions are more complex or seasonal. Email marketing is one of the best ways to nurture leads until they're ready to act and make a purchase. As they become more comfortable with your brand and reliant on the information you send to help solve their problems, save them time, or simply make their lives a bit better, they're also more likely to spread the word about your brand to other people. Email messages are highly shareable, and it takes just a second for a recipient to click the forward button and send your message to another contact. Therefore, email marketing can be an excellent form of word-of-mouth marketing and brand advocacy, too.

Time-Saving

Once you set up your email marketing tool, create some email automation sequences and integrate your email marketing with your website, Google Analytics, and other marketing programs, you can save a significant amount of time on a daily basis. Rather than manually sending thank-you messages, confirmations, offers, and so on to people, you can set everything up in advance, turn it on, and let it run by itself.

It's important to test your automations on an ongoing basis to ensure nothing has gone wrong. No technology is perfect, so it's better to be safe than sorry. Add yourself to your automation lists and see what happens. If something goes wrong, fix it immediately. A poorly developed, written, or configured email message could do far more harm to your business than good.

Disadvantages of Email Marketing

The negative aspects of email marketing should not deter you from using it. Regardless of the challenges, it's still one of the most effective ways of promoting your products and services to consumers and motivating them to take the action you want them to (such as making a purchase). However, it's important to understand the disadvantages so you're not surprised down the road. They include the following.

Deliverability

Two things can affect the deliverability of your email messages. The first is spam. Internet service providers (ISPs) that deliver messages to email inboxes are actively looking for spam, and they'll either stop it before it reaches a recipient or send it to a recipient's spam folder if it's suspicious. Fortunately, there are steps you can take to reduce the risk that your messages will be flagged as spam, which you'll learn more about in Chapter 3. However, the risk is still always there.

The other problem is your email marketing service provider. Not all tools are equal in the "minds" of internet service providers. Some have better reputations than others, and with those better reputations come better deliverability rates. High-quality email service providers take steps to reduce the number of messages they send that are flagged as spam and to ensure ISPs will accept and deliver the messages that come from them. These steps include authentication, using a dedicated domain, getting whitelisted by internet service providers, and more. If your email service provider doesn't work on an ongoing basis to optimize deliverability, then your email marketing results will be negatively affected. With that in mind, make sure you choose a reputable email service provider. You'll be introduced to many of them in Chapter 4.

Clutter

People are inundated with messages every day, and that includes inside their email inboxes. According to Internet Live Stats, as of August 2017, more than 2.6 million email messages are sent per second, and 67 percent of them are spam (www.internetlivestats.com/one-second/). It's hard to stand out!

With that said, it's very easy for people to unsubscribe from your email list, but think of it this way. They can easily look away from your print ad, click away from your online ad, or throw away your direct mail piece. It's the same thing, but with email marketing, you can send highly relevant information—not just promotional messages. Hopefully, interested consumers who might buy one day won't hit the "unsubscribe" button, and those who will never buy can unsubscribe. As a result, you can invest your time and money on those people who will have the potential to drive revenue for your business in the future.

Time Requirements

If you're technically savvy and you can write great email marketing messages, then email marketing can be easy. Not only can you set up automated email marketing campaigns that run without your daily involvement, but you can also create email marketing campaigns any time a new opportunity arises. Furthermore, you can strategize comprehensive email marketing programs that are key components of the integrated marketing plan for your business.

However, there's something important to remember. Email *automation* can save you a lot of time, but email *marketing* can be very time consuming. First, it takes time to set up everything correctly in your email marketing application, on your website, in your opt-in forms, in your lead pages, in your analytics tool, and so on. If you're segmenting your list into smaller groups of people with similar characteristics or behaviors so you can send the most relevant messages possible to them, as discussed in detail in Chapter 9, it's even more time consuming to set up everything correctly. If you're not technically savvy or you're not a copywriter, it will take you even longer to set up and manage your email marketing on an ongoing basis.

Skills

Many people who don't have the necessary skills to set up and manage email campaigns and automations in their email marketing applications have to invest more money to hire someone to do it. If that describes you, then you'll need to find someone to help you set up and/or manage all your email marketing programs for you.

Make sure you hire someone who understands the email marketing application you've chosen. While they're all similar, they offer different advanced features that an email marketer might not be familiar with. For example, the advanced segmentation and automation capabilities of Infusionsoft are extremely different from the capabilities offered by MailChimp. These are important challenges to consider before you hire someone.

Final Thoughts about Email Marketing Pros and Cons

Keeping all the pros and cons you just learned in mind, you could do everything right and still not get the response you want from your email marketing campaigns. Email marketing is not a once-and-done strategy. You should use it to keep your brand top-of-mind without being annoying. That means you need to send useful, meaningful, relevant content to your audience that solves problems, entertains, educates, or motivates them to take some kind of action. See Chapter 10 to learn more about writing email messages your audience wants to receive.

INTRODUCTION TO EMAIL MARKETING TOOLS, PROCESSES, AND TERMINOLOGY

As email marketing has evolved over the years, so have email marketing tools. We've moved from mass email marketing to highly targeted, time-sensitive, and event-triggered email marketing. As spam filters improved and more companies stopped sending unsolicited email messages, consumers discovered that they *want* to hear about promotions, offers, deals, news, and more from companies via email. They're more than willing to opt into brands' email lists to get this valuable information.

Naturally, competition in the email service provider market has grown. Not only are there more companies offering email marketing SaaS tools, but these companies are offering long lists of features within their software applications. All the tools and terminology can get confusing, so before you go any further in this book, take a few minutes to learn the key terms discussed in the remainder of this chapter. Without this knowledge, you could invest time and money into tools you don't need.

ESP vs. Marketing Automation vs. CRM

First, you should understand the difference between an email marketing service provider or email service provider (ESP), marketing automation, and customer relationship management (CRM). These terms are important because the features offered by an ESP are different from those offered by a comprehensive marketing automation tool or a CRM.

Email Service Provider (ESP)

An ESP provides software that enables you to send email messages to lists of people at specific times. You might be able to create multiple lists, segment those lists into smaller groups of people, and even automatically send newsletters and specific campaigns that you create. Typically, the ESP provides easy-to-use design tools so you can create messages that look highly professional. An ESP might even offer great-looking opt-in forms you can use on your website to collect email addresses from new subscribers. Some ESPs include simple automation features that allow you to set up a series of messages, which are automatically sent to people on your list at specific times or after specific behaviors (such as when a recipient clicks on a link in a message).

An *opt-in form* appears on your website and invites visitors to subscribe to receive email updates from you. The form includes a field for visitors to input their email addresses. Depending on the ESP you're using, you might be able to include additional fields in the form such as name and address. Ideally, when visitors subscribe using the opt-in form, their email addresses will automatically be added to your list within your ESP account.

Think of an ESP's software as a tool to build relationships with consumers and make sales. Popular ESPs include MailChimp, Constant Contact, iContact, AWeber, ActiveCampaign, ConvertKit, ClickFunnels and Emma, to name a few.

Marketing Automation

Marketing automation providers have developed software that enables you to do email marketing and much more. Using marketing automation software, you can integrate your email marketing, content marketing, online advertising, and many other marketing efforts so you can track leads from acquisition to conversion. The goal of using this software is to streamline and automate tasks to save time and money. Furthermore, centralizing marketing activities in a marketing automation software improves tracking so you can better identify which tactics perform the best and adjust your marketing budget quickly and efficiently.

Marketing automation is all about lead nurturing and moving consumers through the marketing funnel (discussed in detail in Chapter 2). The software offers advanced segmentation features to ensure highly targeted audiences get the best messages at specific times. The automation features are also very advanced, so a business can run much of its marketing on auto-pilot once it's set up. Popular marketing automation software providers include HubSpot, Marketo, SharpSpring, and Pardot by Salesforce.

Customer Relationship Management (CRM)

A CRM is a sales tool—not a marketing tool (although there is some overlap). CRM software enables you to follow a person's entire lifetime with your business. You can quickly see all of a person's contact information, your interactions with that person, dates and notes about phone conversations, notes about the person's needs and preferences, their purchase history, and more.

The goal of using CRM software is to improve interactions between your business and consumers so they're more likely to buy and to tell other people about how satisfied they are buying from you. Your salespeople can easily track prospects and close more sales when they have all this useful information at their fingertips. Popular CRM software is available from Salesforce, Zoho CRM, Insightly, PipelineDeals, Nimble, and NetSuite CRM.

You'll learn more about email marketing tools throughout this book, and a complete resource list is included in the appendix. For now, don't worry about which tool you'll

SOFTWARE THAT DOES IT ALL

There are some software products available that don't fit neatly into the ESP, marketing automation, or CRM categories because they do a little bit of each. For example, Infusionsoft and Ontraport are excellent tools for email marketing, as well as some marketing automation and CRM. Similarly, ActiveCampaign offers email marketing and marketing automation features with some CRM features included in plans at higher price points. HubSpot offers a marketing automation product and a CRM product, and both include email marketing features.

The best advice is to not worry about semantics. As you read this book, make a list of the features you need in an email marketing tool, then search for software that offers all those features. For most small businesses, this will be an ESP software to start. You might want to graduate to a marketing automation or CRM tool in the future, but an ESP meets most entrepreneur's needs at first.

choose when the time comes. Instead, focus on learning how to use email marketing to grow your business by creating campaigns that work.

Email Automation vs. Drip Email Marketing

Two more terms that can be confusing because they're often used interchangeably are *email automation* and *drip email marketing*. Both these terms refer to the process of automatically sending email messages to people on your list. In other words, you create a sequence of messages and set up specific times or actions that signal the next message in the sequence to be delivered. Here are a few examples:

- When a person subscribes to your email list, your email marketing software is set up to automatically send a thank-you message and put the subscriber into a campaign that automatically sends ("drips") a follow-up message three days later with useful information and links to your social media profiles.
- You send a message through your email marketing software to all your customers promoting a special coupon code that expires in two weeks. Anyone who does not open the message automatically receives a reminder message two days later, and everyone on the list receives a separate reminder message the day before the coupon expires.
- You send your weekly newsletter, which includes information about your new ebook and a downloadable link. If someone clicks on the downloadable link showing they're interested in the ebook topic, they're automatically added to a separate campaign that sends more relevant information and invites them to join your upcoming webinar on the same topic.

Each of these examples could include multiple messages depending on how the campaign sequences are configured in the email marketing software. Bottom-line, email automation (not to be confused with marketing automation) and drip marketing generally mean the same thing. You're automatically dripping messages to people based on timing or behaviors.

THE ROLE OF EMAIL IN AN INTEGRATED MARKETING PLAN

Keep in mind as you read this book, email marketing is effective, but it's not the only marketing tactic you should be using to grow your brand and business. Rather, it's one piece of an integrated marketing plan. Let's take a step back and see what that means.

By definition, integrated marketing attempts to create a seamless brand experience across all marketing channels, including email, social media, advertising, direct mail, point-of-sale, and so on. It focuses on your marketing communications and includes strategies that will be implemented to build your brand based on the three fundamental rules of branding:

1. *Consistency.* All marketing messages and materials must be consistent with the brand promise.
2. *Persistence.* Brands aren't built overnight. You must be persistent in getting your brand messages in front of consumers again and again.
3. *Restraint.* It can be tempting to extend your brand far and wide to build it quickly, but don't follow every opportunity, or you could dilute your brand. If an opportunity doesn't match your brand promise or causes you to lose focus on your brand's purpose, don't pursue it.

> *Integrated marketing* is an approach to creating a seamless brand experience across all marketing channels.

The three fundamental rules of branding are in place for an important reason. They keep you from confusing consumers, and brand confusion is the number-one brand killer. If your brand doesn't meet consumers' expectations for it based on the brand promise, they'll turn away in search of another brand that meets their expectations in every interaction. For example, the messaging you use in your email marketing messages shouldn't be completely different from the messaging you use on your website, on social media, or in your ads. By creating an integrated marketing plan, you'll ensure your marketing messages consistently represent your brand promise across channels and position your brand for growth and loyalty, rather than confusion and abandonment.

Chapter 2

The Marketing Funnel

If you have a business, then you probably already have funnels in place and don't even realize it. For example, if you have a website, you have a funnel. That's because funnels aren't just for marketing, although the vast majority overlap with marketing in some way. Funnel, pipeline, cycle, process—these are all words used to describe different ways to move consumers from awareness to action. By reading this book, you're learning how to create the most effective email campaign funnels and optimize your existing and new funnels to generate conversions and boost your return on investment. With that said, let's take a step back and identify what a funnel is.

A *marketing funnel* is visually represented by the same type of funnel you'd use in cooking or automotive work. It's a conical object with a large hole at the top and a small hole at the bottom. You might use a funnel to pour oil or gasoline from a container into your car. The goal is to get all the oil or gasoline through the funnel so none drips out and doesn't make it into the car. Ideally, a marketing funnel would do the same thing—ensure every person completes a specific action. However, this isn't realistic. The entire consumer audience enters the funnel at the top, but unlike the funnel you use in cooking or when working on your car, not everyone makes it out at the bottom. Filters and holes are along the way.

You *will* end up losing people, but ultimately, your goal is to get as many of the *right* customers for the offer through the funnel so they take action.

A marketing funnel is a theoretical and practical approach to matching marketing strategies and tactics (including email marketing) to consumers' purchasing behaviors. To understand the marketing funnel, you first have to understand the consumer purchasing process.

Let's look at it in a practical sense. Pretend you have an unlimited marketing budget and you want to promote your new product to get people to buy it for the first time. You could buy an ad to play during the Super Bowl. A massive audience will see it, which means a massive audience will get into the top of your marketing funnel. However, it's likely that most of these people are not going to buy your product today or in the future. They're simply not the right match for a long list of reasons. With a marketing funnel, you invest time and money to move people through your funnel until they take action, but no one has the funds to invest in an audience of, well, everyone. Your goal is to maximize the number of people who make it to each stage of the funnel without overpaying for people who are very unlikely to ever complete the final action you want them to take.

Marketers use email messages, content, advertisements, and more to move people through the marketing funnel. Slowly (or quickly, depending on the industry, product, and audience) a large pool of potential customers is whittled into smaller pools until, finally, a group of consumers make it out of the bottom of the funnel and completes the action (such as making a purchase).

The marketing funnel is divided into three parts as shown in Figure 2–1 on page 15: the top, middle, and bottom of the funnel. Different types of messages, content, ads, and so on are used at each stage of the funnel to keep people moving through it.

Top of the Funnel (TOFU)

At the top of the funnel is everyone who isn't close to ready to buy yet. They might not even realize they have a problem or need at this point. Your goal at the top of the funnel is to raise awareness of your product, service, or brand and attract a large number of leads. You want to fill up your funnel.

Middle of the Funnel (MOFU)

People in the middle of the funnel have already started researching product, service, or brand options. They're gathering information to help them make a purchase decision. Throughout this stage of the funnel, they're narrowing down their selections until they've identified a small set of preferred products, services, or

FIGURE 2–1. Marketing Funnel

brands. You want to give them useful information so their interest in what you offer increases even more.

Bottom of the Funnel (BOFU)

People in the bottom of the funnel are very close to acting. It's time for you to directly try to convince your audience to act. For example, this could be where you close the sale or motivate someone to pick up the phone and call you. In other words, people at the bottom of the funnel are ready to hear about your product, service, or brand, so now is the time to promote it. At this stage, it's essential that you communicate with prospects often. They're at the tipping point, and you have to determine what type of messages, content, promotions, or other nurturing will give them the last little push that motivates them to act. Don't worry. You'll get many tips, ideas, and samples in this book that you can use.

EMAIL CONVERSION FUNNEL CAMPAIGNS

This book teaches you about a specific type of marketing funnel—the email conversion funnel. You'll learn how to create email marketing campaigns that successfully lead consumers to take a predetermined action (i.e., convert). The end-goal or desired action might be to increase email subscribers, boost webinar sign-ups, generate free trials, close sales, or something else. The choice is yours. However, it's important to understand that email conversion funnels are usually made up of a lot of parts and pieces—not just a series of email messages.

Depending on your industry, business, products, and services, your email conversion funnel campaigns could include a complicated sequence of automated email messages, landing pages, telephone calls, appointments, free demos, free trials, ebooks, checklists, webinars, and more. You'll learn more about all of that throughout this book, but suffice it to say, email marketing takes a lot of strategizing, setup, monitoring, and follow-up to be successful. It also requires a great deal of testing.

Fortunately, when you can identify where the consumers you're communicating with through your email messages are in the buying cycle and marketing funnel, your campaigns will be more successful. You can see this alignment visually in Figure 2–2 on page 17.

When consumers aren't in the market yet, they're at the top of the funnel, and your email messages should be focused on building awareness. When they start researching options, they've reached the middle of the funnel, and your email messages should be focused on providing useful, meaningful information to help them in their research. Finally, when they're ready to make a purchase decision at the bottom of the funnel, you need to make sure your messages clearly communicate what makes your product, service, or brand the best possible choice. Check out "15 Email Message Ideas for Every Stage of the Marketing Funnel" on page 18 for content suggestions to include in your email marketing messages at each stage of the marketing funnel.

THE CONSUMER BUYING CYCLE

The marketing funnel directly correlates to the consumer buying cycle. The buyer journey has evolved over the years, and marketers and salespeople have had to adjust their communications to adapt. Think of it this way—a person who is just starting to think about replacing their car is probably not even close to making a purchase. They're

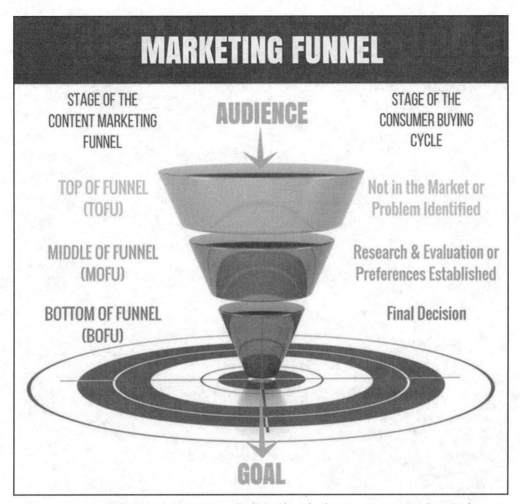

FIGURE 2–2. The Marketing Funnel Aligned with the Consumer Buying Cycle

in the earliest stages of the buying cycle. They've identified that they have a problem, but they're just starting to evaluate their options using the massive amount of information available. People in this stage of the buying cycle need to see and hear different messages and consume different content than people who are ready to buy a new car right now.

As shown in Figure 2–3 on page 19, there are five primary steps in today's Consumer Buying Cycle, which you should consider before creating an email campaign (or any marketing campaign or content).

1. *Not in the market yet.* In Stage 1, the consumer has not identified a problem that has created a want or need. Therefore, they are not in the market for a product or service at all.

15 EMAIL MESSAGE IDEAS FOR EVERY STAGE OF THE MARKETING FUNNEL

Top of the Funnel

1. Educational articles

2. Educational videos

3. Short, introductory ebooks

4. Checklists

5. Worksheets

Middle of the Funnel

1. How-to videos

2. Case studies

3. Product descriptions

4. Long, deep-dive ebooks

5. Webinar replays and presentation slides

Bottom of the Funnel

1. Testimonials

2. Demo videos

3. Product or service reviews

4. Competitor comparison tables

5. Discounts and special promotions

2. *Problem identified.* In Stage 2, the consumer has identified a problem that created a want or need. That problem could be physical or emotional, and the consumer might not actually call it a problem. They are about to enter the market for a product or service to solve the problem.

3. *Research and evaluation.* In Stage 3, the consumer has started conducting research to find solutions to their problem and is evaluating different product or service options.

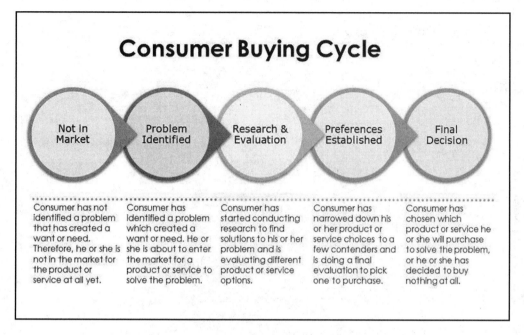

FIGURE 2–3. Consumer Buying Cycle

4. *Preferences established.* In Stage 4, the consumer has narrowed their product or service choices to a few contenders and is doing a final evaluation to pick one to purchase.

5. *Final decision.* In Stage 5, the consumer has chosen which product or service they will purchase to solve the problem, or they have decided to buy nothing.

The type of product or service you offer, your prices, your industry, and a variety of other factors could influence how long it takes for consumers to move through the buying cycle for your business. For example, the process is certainly longer for a car than a candy bar. In addition to these tangible factors, there are many emotional factors that influence consumers' purchasing decisions. Buying decisions are rarely 100 percent rational. As you develop email marketing programs, you also need to understand who your customers are, what makes them tick, and what motivates them physically and emotionally.

Fortunately, while the world has changed around us over the years, people's needs and their behaviors related to satisfying those needs haven't changed as much as you might think. This includes how people make purchase decisions. We're still guided by psychologist Abraham Maslow's Hierarchy of Needs, which he developed in 1943. Maslow identified five human needs and ranked them in a hierarchy as shown in Figure 2–4 on page 20.

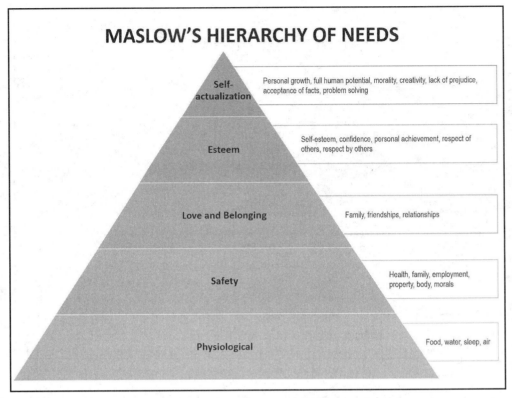

FIGURE 2–4. Maslow's Hierarchy of Needs

At the bottom of the hierarchy are physiological needs. These are the things humans need to survive such as food and water. The second level includes safety needs such as health, family, and a job. These are the needs that give humans a sense of security. Third are love and belonging needs, which are related to relationships, family, and friendships. Notice as you travel up the hierarchy, the needs become less essential for survival and more emotional. The fourth level includes esteem needs such as self-esteem, confidence, respect of and by others, and personal achievement. These needs occur in human beings' conscious and subconscious minds. Finally, the top of the hierarchy is the need for self-actualization, which refers to personal growth and realizing full human potential. This need is very subjective, highly personal, and continually sought but rarely achieved.

Purchase decisions are greatly affected by real and perceived needs. At the bottom of Maslow's hierarchy are items people purchase for real, physical needs. The higher up the hierarchy a consumer goes, the more their needs shift from real to perceived ones. The goal for marketers is to understand each level of needs for a

THE AIDA MODEL

In 1898, an American advertising and sales pioneer by the name of E. St. Elmo Lewis created what would come to be known as the AIDA Model. Based on his analysis of the insurance industry, his simple model focused on four key stages in the consumer lifecycle: awareness, interest, desire, and action (see Figure 2–5). Lewis' model became the cornerstone of sales and marketing, and it was sales and marketing professionals' jobs to develop techniques and campaigns that would successfully move consumers through the AIDA Model until they took the final, desired action—most often, making a purchase.

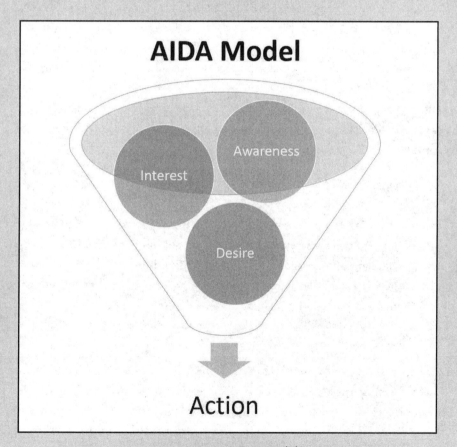

FIGURE 2–5. AIDA Model

THE AIDA MODEL, continued

The AIDA Model theorized that prospects must become *aware* of a product, service, or brand before they can consider purchasing it. Once they're aware of the product, they can develop an *interest* in buying it. After some thought and analysis, they can begin to *desire* a specific product, service, or brand. Ultimately, they'll take *action* and make a purchase. Sales and marketing professionals would work throughout the AIDA process to control consumers' journeys through the four stages using advertising, sales calls, marketing materials, and more.

The AIDA Model was very effective in helping marketers and salespeople understand consumer behavior and the purchase decision-making process. The model defined the buying process in a linear manner, and it enabled companies to better communicate with consumers. Broad advertising and sales cold calls boosted awareness while marketing promotions and sales calls nurtured interest and increased desire until consumers finally acted. The process was simple years ago when consumers weren't bombarded with messages from every direction on a continual basis and didn't have access to so much information at their fingertips.

As you can imagine, Lewis' AIDA Model has evolved over the past century. In fact, it could be argued that the bulk of its transformation occurred in the past 20 years as the internet grew. Today, people enter a funnel like the one pictured in Figure 2–1 (on page 15) at different stages. Similarly, they can drop out of the funnel at many different times. Today's marketers need to think not only of moving consumers through the funnel until they take a specific action but also how to bring them back in when they drop out (and if they *should* bring them back in).

target audience and develop marketing initiatives and messages that clearly address those needs for consumers. The trick is differentiating your products and services from competitors and positioning them as the *only* solution, the *best* choice for the consumer, and the brand the consumer *needs* knowing that most of this need is perception-based (i.e., perceived pain points and problems), not survival based. The way you do this changes depending on where consumers are in the buying cycle and marketing funnel.

CREATING BUYER PERSONAS TO BOOST FUNNEL ROI

Understanding where consumers are in the buying cycle is just one piece of the puzzle to develop effective marketing funnels. You also need to understand *who* your customers are. Before you start creating marketing funnels, you should research your customers and create buyer personas for your ideal customer as well as niche segments of consumers so you can create better email marketing campaigns in the future.

A buyer persona is a written representation of a customer group. Your goal is to identify shared motivations and challenges so you can create marketing offers and messages that will appeal to specific groups of people. Each buyer persona you create represents a segment of your audience based on data that you collect through your research in three specific areas:

- *Demographic characteristics*. The physical and tangible characteristics of a person, such as their age, income, gender, marital status, education, and whether they have children or own a home.
- *Psychographic characteristics*. The emotional and intangible characteristics of a person, such as their beliefs and values. These characteristics are influenced by human psychology.
- *Behavioral characteristics*. The actions a person takes that can be used to identify consumer preferences, such as the type of car a person owns, their hobbies, the websites they visit, the magazines they buy, and the TV shows they watch.

To develop your buyer personas, you can interview customers, prospects, and your competitors' customers. Talk to your sales team, customer service representatives, and anyone else in your organization who has direct contact with your customers and can give insight into their thoughts, feelings, and behaviors. You can also conduct surveys with your current and prospective customers online, by telephone, or by mail.

As you speak with people to learn about their needs, problems, challenges, and motivations, ask as many open-ended questions as you can. The secret sauce to creating effective buyer personas is diving into conversations. From these discussions, you can identify common themes and use those themes to group customers into segments that will become your buyer personas. In addition to demographic, psychographic, and behavioral characteristics, see "13 Areas of Focus to Include in Your Buyer Personas" on page 24 for more areas of focus that you should include in your buyer personas at a minimum.

Once you've collected all the information you need, you can create your buyer personas, which will become your marketable consumer segments. Your email marketing, copywriting, ad placements, content marketing, social media marketing, and more will

13 AREAS OF FOCUS TO INCLUDE IN YOUR BUYER PERSONAS

1. *Demographics*. Age, ethnicity, gender, etc.

2. *Psychographics*. Values, beliefs, etc.

3. *Behaviors*. Hobbies, TV shows they watch, brands they buy, etc.

4. *Pain points*. Money, time, ease of use, etc. Think of the emotional triggers that affect each audience.

5. *Problems*. What problems are consumers trying to solve by buying a product or service like yours? What problems is your product or service capable of solving that consumers might not realize they have?

6. *Differentiators*. Why should consumers buy from your business? Be sure to include quantifiable differentiators.

7. *Information sources*. Where do consumers get information that influences their buying decisions for products or services in your category? This could be websites, word-of-mouth recommendations, TV, industry periodicals, etc.

8. *Engagement*. What level of engagement do consumers typically have with you? This could range from no engagement all the way to brand advocacy where they talk about your brand, promote it, and defend it to other people.

9. *Attitudes and concerns*. What attitudes or concerns prevent consumers from buying a product or service like yours (from you and/or from anyone else)?

10. *Outcomes*. What results do consumers want to get when they buy your product or a product like yours?

11. *Features*. What features of your product are most important to consumers?

12. *Benefits*. What benefits of your product are most important to consumers?

13. *Decision making*. Do they make the decision to buy a product or service like yours, or is another person the decision-maker?

vary based on which personas you're speaking with and where consumers are in the buying cycle and the marketing funnel. Clearly, messages for a teen girl's buyer persona would often be very different from messages for a male senior citizen's buyer persona. Of course, your buyer personas will be more complex, but you get the idea. You have to speak to each buyer persona in their preferred language and tailor your content and offer to them appropriately, or your results will suffer. You can do it very effectively through segmented email marketing.

As you develop your buyer personas, be careful to avoid common segmentation mistakes. For example, effective market segmentation is not a once-and-done activity. You need to continually analyze your segments as well as the overall market to ensure your segmentation is still valid. You also need to be careful not to create segments that are too broad, or they won't help you. Similarly, segments that are too narrow can deliver a negative return on your investment simply because it's too expensive to market to them. Also, don't let yourself become a victim of information paralysis. Getting lost in the data might cause you to miss the most important details, or worse, it could keep you from moving forward. Finally, don't let size fool you. Just because an audience segment is the largest doesn't mean it will be the most profitable.

> **Buyer Persona Worksheet**
> Visit www. ultimateguideto emailmarketing .com/bpw to download a free Buyer Persona Worksheet you can use to develop your own buyer personas.

BRINGING IT ALL TOGETHER FOR EMAIL MARKETING

Think about how your email marketing can align with the marketing funnel and consumer buying cycle as well as how you can make your messages more appealing to recipients by leveraging buyer personas. Rather than sending a message with a 15 percent discount to a broad audience of people at the top of the funnel who may not be interested or might have bought anyway without the discount, you should save that discount to use in messages sent to people in the bottom of the funnel who need that final extra push to buy. In addition, rather than sending a message containing a basic, educational article to people who are at the purchase decision stage of the consumer buying cycle, you should be sending them demo videos and testimonials.

Similarly, rather than sending a generic competitor comparison table to consumers at the bottom of the funnel who are ready to make a purchase decision, you should send tables that are customized to each person's buyer persona. It's highly likely that different people will be motivated by different features and benefits. Your conversion numbers will go up if that competitor comparison table is tailored to each person's physical and emotional needs.

These are just a few examples to consider as you learn about email campaign conversion funnels. Always remember, there is a great deal of strategy behind every marketing funnel. Return to this chapter whenever you need a refresher.

Chapter 3

Know the Laws and Deliverability Rules

As an email marketer, you need to comply with laws that were put in place to protect consumers. While it might be tempting to buy a list of email addresses and just start sending messages to everyone on that list, this is a bad idea for a few reasons. First, you might be breaking the law. Second, you might be hurting your chances of your future email marketing messages getting into people's email inboxes, including inboxes belonging to your own customers. The bottom line is your actions as an email marketer can affect the deliverability of your email today and in the future.

Believe it or not, the vast majority of email doesn't make it to people's inboxes. Return Path's "2015 Email Deliverability Benchmark Report" revealed that 21 percent of emails that people have opted-in to receive never make it to an inbox. That means more than one in five people don't get the messages they asked to receive. Clearly, following the written laws and unwritten rules of email marketing is critical to securing a positive return on your investments. The

Definition
Email marketing is an important form of *permission marketing*. In simplest terms, permission marketing is any form of consumer communications where companies should obtain permission from individuals before contacting them. Just as companies should obtain permission to call consumers on the telephone, they also should obtain permission to send commercial email messages to consumers.

most important law you need to know and follow in the United States is the CAN-SPAM Act of 2003.

THE CAN-SPAM ACT OF 2003

Different countries have their own laws related to email marketing. For example, the U.S., Canada, and the European Union each have laws that affect what businesses can send to consumers via email. In the U.S., the law you need to understand and adhere to is the CAN-SPAM Act of 2003. This law applies to all forms of commercial email messages and not just commercial email messages sent in bulk to lists of people.

> **Definition**
>
> The *CAN-SPAM Act* defines commercial messages as "any electronic mail message, the primary purpose of which is the commercial advertisement or promotion of a commercial product or service."

What makes a message commercial? It's not clearly defined in the law, but it's probably broader than you think. For example, a message doesn't have to promote a product or service directly to be considered commercial. Even messages that promote content on a commercial website—such as a blog post, free ebook, educational article, or tutorial—would be considered commercial since they indirectly promote the company. It doesn't matter if you're sending messages to your current customers, former customers, or newsletter subscribers who have never had a customer relationship with you. If the message is considered commercial, you must comply with the CAN-SPAM Act.

The cost for noncompliance can be very high, particularly since you can be charged penalties for each separate email violation up to $40,654. Furthermore, if your email messages violate other laws, such as those related to deceptive advertising, you could face even more fines or criminal penalties, including imprisonment. Ignorance is not an acceptable defense in the eyes of the law, so do your homework and familiarize yourself with the CAN-SPAM Act and other business laws.

Keep in mind, even transactional messages confirming a purchase or shipment could be considered commercial if they contain more commercial content than transactional and must comply with the CAN-SPAM Act of 2003. There are seven primary requirements of the CAN-SPAM Act. Following is a basic explanation of each of the main requirements. If you always err on the side of caution and assume messages sent from your company are commercial advertisements or promotions (even if they're not directly advertising or promoting a product or service), then you should be safe.

TEN EXAMPLES OF COMMERCIAL MESSAGES PER THE CAN-SPAM ACT

1. Announcing your new product

2. Promoting your new blog post

3. Including a link to download your free ebook

4. Sharing a link to your product tutorial video

5. Announcing your upcoming free webinar

6. Promoting a discount or coupon

7. Describing new features offered through your product or service

8. Announcing you'll be at an upcoming trade show or event

9. Asking people to like your business or product Facebook Page or follow you on Twitter or another social media channel

10. Sharing details from your new study or report

Header Information

The header information in your messages must not be false or misleading. This includes the information in the message's "From," "To," and "Reply-To" fields as well as the routing information. In other words, your messages should accurately identify both the person and business that initiated the message. Furthermore, the header information should include the originating domain (which is typically your business' web domain) and real email address.

> **Definition**
>
> A *domain* includes a name and suffix, such as Google.com or Microsoft. com.

Subject Line

The subject line of your email messages must reflect the true content of the message. Don't try to conceal what the message is about with a clever subject line. Instead, the subject line should clearly explain what the recipient will get when they open the message. Both inaccurate and vague subject lines could get you in trouble.

Ad Disclosure

You must identify that the message is an ad or promotional in nature. The good news is that the CAN-SPAM Act provides a great deal of flexibility in terms of how you disclose this information. The most important thing to understand is that somewhere in your message, you must conspicuously explain that your message is promotional (even if it's indirectly promotional) or an advertisement. Leave no room for confusion here.

Location

You must include your physical address in your messages. This has to be your valid postal address, which means it can be your street address or a post office box registered with the U.S. Postal Service. It could also be a private mailbox that you registered with a commercial mail receiving agency, but make sure that agency was established under postal service regulations or it won't meet the requirements of the CAN-SPAM Act.

Unsubscribe Option

Your messages must include an easy and obvious way to unsubscribe if recipients want to opt out of receiving email messages from you in the future. You cannot create conditions to opt out, such as requiring a person to pay a fee or provide any personally identifiable information aside from an email address. Furthermore, the opt-out process must not require a person to do more than send a reply email message or visit one web page. If you send multiple types of messages (e.g., newsletters, product updates, and so on), you can offer a way for people to choose which types of email messages they want to opt out of receiving from you. However, you must also provide a way for them to opt out of receiving *all* messages from you.

Opt-Out Completion

After you send a message, recipients must have 30 days to unsubscribe. If someone unsubscribes, you must honor that request within 10 business days. Once a person unsubscribes, you're not allowed to transfer or sell that person's email address (individually or as part of a list) to anyone else (unless the company you're transferring the list to is helping you comply with the CAN-SPAM Act).

Third Parties

If you hire another person or company to manage your email marketing, you're still responsible for complying with the CAN-SPAM Act. In fact, both you and the person or company handling your email marketing are responsible and could get in trouble

> ## WHERE TO LEARN MORE ABOUT THE LAWS
>
> Learn more about the CAN-SPAM Act at https://www.ftc.gov/tips-advice/business-center/guidance/can-spam-act-compliance-guide-business.
>
> Learn more about advertising and marketing laws at https://www.ftc.gov/tips-advice/business-center/advertising-and-marketing.

if the law isn't followed. Therefore, make sure anyone you work with knows the laws and complies with them. You'll need to monitor their activities for compliance on an ongoing basis.

UNDERSTANDING THE IMPORTANCE OF EMAIL DELIVERABILITY

Just because you hit the send button doesn't mean the people on your email list will receive your messages. In fact, even if they've opted in to receive messages from you, studies show that for every five opt-in messages sent, at least one doesn't make it to people's inboxes. You don't want that to be your message. That's why understanding the factors that affect email deliverability is so important. Sending messages that never land in the intended recipients' inboxes is a waste of time and money.

First, consider the path your messages take to get to recipients' inboxes. It's filled with obstacles put in place by internet service providers (ISPs) that have a single goal in mind—to keep spam out of their customers' inboxes. When you send your messages, your ISP sends them to recipients' ISPs, such as Google, Yahoo, Comcast, and so on. The receiving ISP has a long list of filtering processes in place to analyze incoming messages for potential spam. If one or more of these flags are detected, the message is flagged as spam and goes directly to the recipient's spam or junk folder.

Even if you're sending legitimate messages that people have opted in to receive, your messages could end up being undelivered because they triggered a spam filter. Look through your own email spam folder. What do you see? If you subscribe to a lot of email newsletters, chances are one or more messages from sites you've subscribed to or companies you've purchased products from are sitting in your spam folder unread. Why? Your ISP detected an element within those messages that triggered them to be flagged as spam. You must mark those messages as "not spam" to train your ISP not to recognize them as spam. Otherwise, they'll keep going into your spam folder. The same thing happens to your email marketing messages (and possibly your transactional messages) if you're not continually monitoring your email deliverability.

How to Improve Your Email Deliverability

Fortunately, you can improve your email deliverability. If you're working with a reputable email service provider (ESP) to send your email marketing messages, it's highly likely the company has a wide variety of processes to improve email deliverability. Do your research and make sure this is the case before you choose your provider. Don't simply believe claims of "99 percent deliverability" or similar deliverability rates. Instead, read the rest of this chapter, make sure you understand the factors that affect deliverability, and then do your due diligence and make sure the provider has appropriate processes in place.

Reducing the chances that your messages are flagged as spam by ISP filters requires following the law and taking steps to make your messages as authentic as possible. The remainder of this chapter focuses on many of the factors that directly affect whether ISPs will see your messages as spam or not, so take some time to review and improve each to boost your email deliverability rates.

Reputation

The reputation of the IP address and domain that you're sending email messages from is one of the first things ISPs look at when determining whether your messages are spam. Your IP address is the numeric address of your device on a network. It is used to identify

WHAT'S THE DIFFERENCE BETWEEN AN ESP AND AN ISP?

As noted earlier in the book, an ESP is an email service provider. This is the company that provides your email marketing software, sends your email marketing messages for you, tracks your results, and so on. An ISP is an internet service provider. This is the company that provides email accounts and message accessibility to people. For example, you might use MailChimp as your ESP to send, automate, and track email marketing campaigns to your subscribers list on behalf of your company or brand, but you might use Comcast or Verizon to send and receive your personal email messages or a web-based email host such as Gmail or Yahoo!.

you and allow you to communicate with others across the network. If you're using an ESP such as ActiveCampaign, GetResponse, MailChimp, or AWeber to send your email marketing messages, then those messages are sent using the ESP's IP address. In this case, the IP is shared among many users, so the behaviors of one user could affect the deliverability of other users' messages.

In simpler terms, if you use MailChimp as your email marketing application and another MailChimp user consistently sends out spam, but MailChimp doesn't catch and stop that user, then the IP address's reputation could be negatively affected. As a result, the deliverability of all messages sent from that IP address will decrease, which means your messages have a greater chance of going to spam folders rather than inboxes. That's why it's so important to choose an ESP that uses multiple IP addresses and continually works to maintain high deliverability rates, which includes blocking accounts that send spam.

When your messages are sent, the receiving ISP checks the reputation of the sender's IP address. If you're using a dedicated IP address (meaning only one sender or company uses that IP address), then it's up to you to build your IP address's reputation. Until ISPs can detect that your IP address sends legitimate messages on a consistent basis, they'll throttle your messages, which means they will go to the spam folder. That's why it's important to warm up your IP address by sending a low volume of messages consistently to build your reputation. Once you've developed a reputation, you can increase the volume, but if you suddenly send a large volume of messages from a random IP address, ISPs will think you're a spammer. Improving your IP address's reputation after it has been tarnished isn't easy.

The reputation of the domain name you're sending messages from also affects deliverability. Your domain name is the name you've registered online (e.g., my company's domain is keysplashcreative.com and my blog's domain is womenonbusiness.com). Even if you're using an ESP to send your email marketing messages, your domain name is still detected through the authentication process discussed in the next section of this chapter. Your domain's reputation is affected by how often messages from your domain go into spam folders due to content or IP address reputation problems vs. how many times messages go into inboxes as well as by how many times recipients mark your messages as spam vs. how many times your messages that landed in recipients' spam folders were marked as not spam. You'll learn more about recipient behaviors later in this chapter. For now, understand that domain reputation affects the deliverability of your email messages.

Authentication and Infrastructure

Authenticating your email address is an important step to ensure your messages are delivered. In simplest terms, authentication allows ISPs to verify the sender's identity and tells the ISP you really are who you claim to be. Most ESPs handle authentication for you using one or more of the three primary authentication methods: Sender Policy Framework (SPF), DomainKeys Identified Mail (DKIM), or Domain-based Message Authentication, Reporting & Conformance (DMARC).

Authenticating your email address helps build your domain reputation and protects you from spammers who use forged email addresses to send phishing and spoofing campaigns. Once you authenticate your email address, you need to update your email domain's DNS (domain name systems) records, TXT (text) records, and MTA (mail transfer agent) records with your hosting provider. Every hosting provider has different instructions to accomplish this, so if you plan to authenticate your email address yourself, check with your provider to learn how to do it. Also, you can use your own authentication even if you're using an ESP, so contact your ESP's support team to learn how to do it.

List Quality

The quality of your email list can significantly affect the deliverability of your email messages. Therefore, list cleansing is a critical practice you should be doing on an ongoing basis. You also need to make sure you follow the law and send email only to people who have opted in to receive messages from you. That means you need to honor unsubscribe requests on a timely basis, too.

WHERE TO GET SPF, DKIM, OR DMARC RECORDS

To get an SPF record for your email address, visit these sites:

- *OpenSPF.org*: www.openspf.org
- *SPFwizard.net*: www.spfwizard.net

To get a DKIM record for your email address, visit these sites:

- *DKIM.org*: www.dkim.org
- *SocketLabs.com*: www.socketlabs.com/domainkey-dkim-generation-wizard

To get a DMARC record for your email address, visit these sites:

- *DMARC.org*: https://dmarc.org/resources/deployment-tools
- *GlobalCyberAlliance.org*: https://dmarc.globalcyberalliance.org

You can maintain a quality email list in several ways. First, make sure people opt in to receive messages from you. Not only is required by many ESPs to get permission before emailing people, but opting in ensures people know who you are. If they recognize you as the sender in their email inboxes, they're less likely to flag your messages as spam. Second, make sure you send messages to your list on a consistent basis. If people forget who you are, they're more likely to mark your messages as spam the next time you email them.

Third, you need to clean your list regularly by removing addresses that delivered hard bounces (meaning there is something wrong with the email address, so messages cannot be delivered to it at all), addresses of subscribers who haven't opened your messages within the past year (you can change this to six months if you send messages on a weekly basis or more frequently), or addresses that are obviously fake or generic, such as admin@domain.com or test@test.com. Each of these types of address problems can negatively affect your sender reputation.

While it might seem like a good idea to keep as many people on your email list as possible, that's not the case when some or many of those addresses are hurting the overall deliverability of your messages. Set up a process to monitor hard bounces and inactive subscribers, and cleanse your list monthly.

Fourth, you must avoid spam traps. You only have to send a message to one spam trap to immediately hurt your reputation. You should avoid two types of spam traps. The first is a recycled spam trap and typically happens to senders who don't maintain quality lists by cleansing them on an ongoing basis. These are email addresses that were valid and belonged to someone at one time but have since been abandoned and become spam addresses. Sending to recycled spam trap addresses shows ISPs that your list quality is low. As a result, your reputation suffers and your deliverability goes down.

The second type of spam trap is the honeypot spam trap, which is also called the pristine spam trap. These email addresses never belonged to anyone. ISPs create them with one goal in mind—to catch spammers who use robots to crawl websites for email addresses (ISPs hide these addresses on websites for this purpose) or to catch people who purchase lists that include these addresses. If you send a message to one of these spam addresses, ISPs know you're sending messages to people you haven't gotten permission to email. As a result, your messages are automatically marked as spam and your reputation tanks.

Content

The content of your messages plays a smaller role in your message deliverability these days than it used to, but that doesn't mean it's not important. Ideally, you should take every step possible to keep your messages from being flagged by ISPs or recipients as

SINGLE OR DOUBLE OPT-IN—WHICH SHOULD YOU USE?

The great debate between whether email marketers should use double or single opt-in when collecting subscriber email addresses has been going on for many years. Only you can decide which you'll use based on your goals.

Single opt-in is the simplest opt-in process. You publish a subscription form online and ask people to submit their email addresses to subscribe to your list. After they type in their email addresses and hit the subscribe button, they're done. That's all there is to it. They're on your list and you can send them your email marketing messages.

Double opt-in adds a second step to the subscription process. After subscribers enter their email addresses and hit the subscribe button on your online form, they receive an email message asking them to verify their subscription. When they open the message, they're told to click on a link to complete the verification. If they don't click that link, they won't get on your email list. If they do click the link, then they're on your list and you can email them in the future.

Using single opt-in will undoubtedly increase the number of subscribers on your list since it's inevitable that every person who submits your subscription form won't click the verification link in a subsequent double opt-in email message. However, with single-opt in, you will get fake email addresses on your list. If you don't cleanse your list, those fake addresses could negatively affect your sender reputation when they bounce. Furthermore, user engagement with your messages is typically higher among double opt-in audiences, which can impact your deliverability rates. (You'll learn more about how recipient behaviors affect deliverability later in this chapter.)

The bottom line is whether you choose to use single or double opt-in is up to you and depends on whether you want a larger list or a more engaged list. There is no right or wrong way to set up your opt-in process, so try testing both to see which drives the best results for you based on your goals.

spam. Therefore, adhere to the following list of email content best practices dos and don'ts to avoid triggering spam filters or complaints:

- Do send content that is relevant to recipients.
- Do send messages that include more text than images.
- Do send messages with well-formatted HTML.

- Do send messages that include an easy-to-see unsubscribe link.
- Do send messages with a familiar sender name that recipients will recognize.
- Don't send messages with embedded forms (include links to forms instead).
- Don't send messages with Flash, JavaScript, or videos (link to those elements instead).
- Don't send messages with attachments.
- Don't use spam trigger words, particularly in your subject line (visit http://ultimateguidetoemailmarketing.com/stw for a list of spam trigger words to avoid in your email messages).
- Don't use URL shorteners in your messages.
- Don't use all caps or excessive punctuation.

None of these best practices are difficult to follow, so always review your messages against this list before you hit the send button. It just takes a few seconds to confirm your content doesn't include any spam flags, and your message deliverability will improve when you eliminate these elements.

Recipient Behaviors

What people do after they receive your messages can greatly affect the deliverability of your messages in the future. For example, if they mark your messages as spam, your sender reputation goes down. That's why it's so important that you consistently email relevant content to your subscribers. However, there is more to how recipient behaviors affect your message deliverability than whether they mark your messages as spam.

> **Definition**
> A *URL shortener* is a tool used to shorten the URL of a web page so it uses fewer characters. Some URL shorteners also offer click tracking. Examples of URL shortener tools are Bitly.com and Goo.gl.

ISPs review how recipients engage with email sent from your IP address. For example, they look at the addresses on your list to determine if the owners of those addresses are real, trustworthy people who actively use their email accounts by logging in, sending, and receiving messages, and even how often they flag messages as spam or not spam. They also analyze recipients' engagement with your messages based on many factors, such as whether they read your messages, move your messages to different folders, forward your messages, reply to your messages, click links in your messages, mark your messages as spam or not spam, add your address to their address books, and more.

Recipient engagement matters a lot to the future deliverability of your messages, but you need to make sure your messages get to subscribers' inboxes in the first place. A great way to do that is to ask your subscribers to add your email address to their personal safe sender lists (also called whitelists) within their email applications. When someone submits your web form and subscribes to your list, display a thank-you page that asks them to add your address to their safe sender lists. You can also include this request in the first email message you send to them, such as your double opt-in verification message or a welcome message. It's also a great idea to remind them to whitelist your email address by including a link to a web page that provides instructions on how to do it with common mail providers like Gmail, Yahoo!, and Outlook.

Blacklists

There are hundreds of blacklists used by ISPs to filter out spam and unwanted email messages, but there are just two main types of blacklists—IP address-based blacklists and domain-based blacklists. IP address-based lists query IP addresses in real-time to find spammers. Domain-based lists search for URLs (including redirects) within the content of email messages to find domains that have been identified as spam sources.

> **Definition**
>
> An *email blacklist* is a database of IP addresses or domains that are known to send spam messages.

If you land on a blacklist, your messages could be blocked by certain ISPs. The extent of the damage depends on how many ISPs use the list. Some lists are used by most ISPs while others are small, private lists. It is possible to get removed from blacklists if you have a good sender reputation and agree to change any questionable email practices you've been using. A few sites you can use to check if you appear on any blacklists are provided below:

- *Uribl*: http://uribl.com
- *Surbl*: www.surbl.org
- *Spamhaus*: www.spamhaus.org
- *MultiRBL*: http://multirbl.valli.org

Most list holders provide forms on their websites that you can use to request removal. For example, to request removal from the Spamhaus list, you need to visit https://www.spamhaus.org/lookup/ and enter your IP address or domain name into the provided form to confirm you're on the blacklist. If the results show you're on the list, a link is provided to request removal. Be sure to clean up any problems with your email marketing practices before you request removal from any blacklist.

Who's Responsible for Email Deliverability?

If you're using an ESP for your email marketing, you might be tempted to assume the ESP is handling all the necessary steps to ensure your messages are delivered. Don't make that mistake because the truth is your ESP's responsibility as it relates to deliverability is very limited. Most important, they're responsible for ensuring the technology they provide is compliant with current laws. While not a responsibility, it's also in their best interest (if they want to keep and attract new customers) to proactively implement functionality and processes that improve deliverability, such as authentication.

It's your responsibility as a sender to comply with the law. It's also in your best interest to send relevant content to your subscribers on a consistent basis to reduce the chances that they'll flag your messages as spam. If you don't invest time and attention into creating useful and meaningful email campaigns, segmenting your subscriber audience so the most relevant messages go to the most appropriate audiences, and cleansing your subscriber list, your deliverability rate will suffer.

Ideally, your efforts to improve your reputation combined with your ESP's efforts to improve deliverability for all its customers should keep your deliverability rate high. If you see your deliverability rate suddenly take a dive, reach out to your ESP for help. Remember, if people don't get your messages, you're wasting your time and money by sending them.

Chapter 4

Choosing Your Tools

Once you've decided to invest some time and money into building your own list of prospects and customers to boost your business through email marketing, you need to choose the tools you'll use to collect those email addresses and send your messages. Many different email marketing tools are available today. Many offer very similar features with smaller nuances that could motivate you to choose one over another. On page 42, you'll find a list of "15 Popular Email Marketing Tools" to start your research.

Keep in mind that ESPs frequently update their tools, so do your research before you buy to ensure you're getting the most current information and pricing. The tool you choose depends very much on your goals for your email marketing investment. Do you just want to collect email addresses and send the same monthly newsletter to everyone? Might you want to send messages based on your subscribers' individual behaviors in the future? Do you want to offer free ebooks or checklists to your website visitors in exchange for their email addresses and automatically send them a link to that free content after they submit a form on your website?

Your answers to these questions affect which email marketing tool you need to use. For example, if you simply want to send the same

15 POPULAR EMAIL MARKETING TOOLS

Here are 15 well-known email marketing providers to start your research. Note that this list does not include marketing automation and CRM tools, which also provide email marketing functionality. Instead, it only includes tools that focus on email marketing. Some may offer CRM features as add-ons, too.

1. ActiveCampaign: www.activecampaign.com
2. AWeber: http://aweber.com
3. Campaign Monitor: www.campaignmonitor.com
4. Click Funnels: www.clickfunnels.com
5. Constant Contact: www.constantcontact.com
6. ConvertKit: https://convertkit.com
7. Drip: www.drip.co
8. Emma: https://myemma.com
9. GetResponse: www.getresponse.com
10. iContact: www.icontact.com
11. Infusionsoft: www.infusionsoft.com
12. Mad Mimi: https://madmimi.com
13. MailChimp: https://mailchimp.com
14. Ontraport: https://ontraport.com
15. VerticalResponse: www.verticalresponse.com

monthly newsletter to everyone who subscribes to your list and have no plans to ever use more sophisticated email marketing tactics to grow your business, then MailChimp will probably meet your needs. However, if you want to send highly targeted messages based on subscribers' interactions with your messages, your website, and more, then you need a different tool, such as the one provided by ActiveCampaign or ConvertKit.

Therefore, sit down and document your short- and long-term email marketing goals. While switching from one ESP to another can be done, it's cumbersome and rarely a perfect process. You don't need to invest in the most sophisticated and expensive email marketing tool today, but make sure you choose a tool that will meet your needs for the foreseeable future. For example, you might just want to send the same weekly newsletter to your entire list today, but in the future, you might want to segment your list into smaller groups with similar characteristics. A health coach might want to send a different newsletter to people who are interested in weight loss than an audience interested in diabetes management. The coach might even release new products or services specific to each of those audiences and want to send promotional offers to convince specific audiences to buy. If the email marketing tool chosen by the health coach today doesn't offer adequate segmentation features, the coach would have to switch to a new tool to pursue their marketing and business growth goals.

There are five key factors that you should consider when choosing a provider for your email marketing: contact management, message design and setup, content and delivery, email management, and account administration and support. The rest of this chapter provides details about each of these factors so you can compare ESPs side-by-side and choose the best one for your business.

1. CONTACT MANAGEMENT

When choosing an email marketing tool, you need one that makes it easy for you to collect subscribers' email addresses legally and to identify who's who within your subscriber list so you always send the right people the appropriate messages. Let's talk about some of the features to consider.

Opt-In Forms

How do you get email addresses to add to your list from people you don't know? You need an opt-in form (or multiple opt-in forms) where, at minimum, you ask people to provide their email addresses. You could also ask for potential subscribers' names or other personal information. This information should automatically be added to your list by your email marketing tool so you don't have to do any of the work manually.

It's important to choose a tool that enables you to create subscription forms that look good. A very simple subscription form created with MailChimp is shown in Figure 4–1 on page 44, but these forms could get as elaborately designed as you want if you have the coding skills to customize them.

Your opt-in rate will go up with a form that looks great versus a form that looks bad. Therefore, make sure you use a tool that either provides professional-looking opt-in forms, allows you to customize the code for your opt-in forms so you or a designer can make them look exactly like you want them to, or easily integrates with a separate

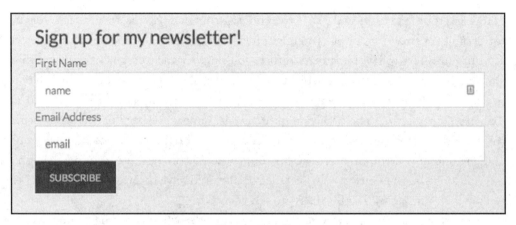

FIGURE 4–1. Simple Email Opt-In Form

application that offers high quality opt-in forms, such as OptinMonster (http://optinmonster.com) or Sumo (https://sumo.com).

Double and Single Opt-In Functionality

As you learned in Chapter 3, single opt-in subscription forms simply require subscribers to enter their email addresses into your form, click a button, and they're done. Double opt-in forms require some extra steps. Most often, the subscriber will receive an email message after they submit the subscription form as shown in the example created with MailChimp in Figure 4–2. The message includes a link that the person must click to verify the subscription. If the person doesn't click the link in that message, they don't get added to your email list.

Ideally, you want an email marketing provider that offers both double and single opt-in functionality so you have maximum flexibility. To recruit new subscribers, you

FIGURE 4–2. Double Opt-In Subscription Confirmation Email Message

might want to use double opt-in to ensure you have unquestionable permission to send marketing messages to them. However, there may be times when you don't want to require double opt-in. If you haven't read Chapter 3, go back and read it now to learn the pros and cons of single vs. double opt-in. The point is, it's best to choose an email tool that is agile enough to meet your ongoing needs, and this agility should apply to the opt-in requirements process, too.

Contact Management Methods

Once you have collected email addresses, the next thing you need to think about is how you're going to keep track of those email addresses so you send the right messages to the right people at the right times. Your email marketing tool should provide you with easy-to-use tools to manage all your contacts for this purpose. Email marketing providers offer two primary ways for you to manage subscribers: list-based and subscriber-based.

List-Based Contact Management

List-based contact management means everything in your email marketing account relies on lists of contacts. When a new contact is added manually or automatically through a form submission, that contact must be placed into a specific list. All messages that you send are based on the lists you create. For example, you might create a list of people who subscribed to your weekly newsletter, a list of people who requested information about your products from your website, a list of people who requested a copy of your free ebook, and so on.

In a list-based system, the same contact could appear on multiple lists. It's up to you to remember what all those lists were for and make sure you choose all the appropriate lists every time you send an email campaign. When someone submits an opt-in form, they're added to one or more lists depending on how you set up the form in your email marketing tool.

For example, a person might submit a form to subscribe to your weekly newsletter. As a result, that person will be on your Weekly Newsletter List. Later, they might submit a form to download your new free ebook, and they'll end up on your Free Ebook list, too. If you decide to send a promotional campaign announcing a discount off a new product in the future and you want that message to go to all your contacts, you'll need to send it to both of your lists to ensure you capture everyone. Unfortunately, that means some people might get your message twice, and not all email marketing providers automatically remove duplicates when you send messages to multiple lists. Again, that means people on multiple lists could get the same message multiple times.

Subscriber-Based Contact Management

Lists are the cornerstone of email marketing, but they're not perfect. Marketing automation tools such as SharpSpring, Marketo, and HubSpot use *tags* to manage contacts rather than lists. Think of it this way. A list is like a giant file cabinet where all your customers' contact information is included without any kind of organization. You could buy multiple file cabinets to hold many different customers' contact information. However, if customers are just thrown into those file cabinets with no organization, it can be very hard to find specific groups of customers when you want to communicate with them. That's where tags make everything easier.

Tags are like the folders in a large filing cabinet. Just as you could create folders to group similar customers together within your large filing cabinet, you can add tags to contact records in your marketing automation tool so it's easy to find them and send them the right marketing offers in the future. A customer could be filed in multiple folders in your filing cabinet based on specific characteristics or behaviors (e.g., everyone who purchased a specific product and who visited the pricing page on your website), which correlates to having multiple tags in your marketing automation software. When you need to find customers with a specific tag, you filter your list of contacts and you're done. You can send email marketing messages to all your contacts who have one or more tags of your choice whenever you want to.

> **Definition**
>
> *Tags* are identifiers you add to contact records to easily find smaller segments of your email marketing list.

Some email marketing providers like ActiveCampaign, Infusionsoft, Ontraport, and ConvertKit offer hybrid email marketing, marketing automation, and customer relationship management solutions so you can manage your email marketing contacts using tags. These tags are used to identify contact actions and behaviors, and they make it much easier to send specific messages to laser-focused audiences. In other words, tags, a sophisticated marketing automation feature, can be found in several hybrid email marketing platforms at more affordable prices than typical marketing automation tools cost.

Rather than using multiple lists, you create just one list and select whom to send messages to based on the tags that have been applied to each contact. For example, you'd have your master list of contacts, and based on how people interact with your subscription forms and email messages, tags can automatically (or manually) be applied to give you more details about each contact's preferences and activities. You can create tags to identify where a contact is in the marketing funnel as you learned in Chapter 2, to identify links the contact clicked that show they're interested in your products, or to identify newsletters they've subscribed to.

Tags are very flexible and make it quick and easy to segment your list of contacts. However, you must be very careful not to let your tags get out of control. If you don't know what they're for and why you created them, they won't help you. Furthermore, a drawback of using tags with just one contact list is the unsubscribe process. If a contact clicks the unsubscribe link in one of your email messages, they will be unsubscribed from your list and will receive no messages from you in the future regardless of your tags. That is because unsubscribes are based on lists—not tags.

A work-around that many top marketers use is to include a short message at the end of every email. For example, if a web design company sends a message to its contacts about its new Facebook advertising services, it could include a snippet of copy at the end of its email message saying, "If you're not interested in Facebook advertising, click here and you'll be removed from these messages, but don't worry! You'll still receive our other useful emails." It's not a perfect solution, but it's a popular option if you want to use tags rather than lists to power your email marketing.

Segmentation

Without a doubt, your email marketing tool must make it easy for you to segment your list. If you use list-based email marketing management, the provider should offer ways to segment your lists based on contact characteristics or behaviors, and if you use subscriber-based email marketing management, then consider looking for a provider that allows you to segment your contacts *within* your tags. The purpose of segmentation is to break your contacts into groups of people with similar interests, demographics, or behaviors so you can send highly targeted messages to them. For example, if you own a pet supply store, it would make sense to segment your list when you're sending an offer applicable to dog owners only.

Segmentation is also important as you build email conversion funnels for moving contacts to make a purchase. You'll learn more about developing campaign conversion funnels in Chapter 8, but for now, understand that you want to choose a tool that enables you to segment your contacts based on who has shown interest in your offers in the past. For example, if you send a campaign offering a discount on dog food, people who open the message but don't click the link to learn more about the discount could become one segment while people who opened the message and clicked the link but didn't buy could be another segment. Their varied levels of interaction with your message imply how far they are through the marketing funnel, and you can create future messages to successfully push them further through that funnel to make a purchase. Bottom line, if you're going to be serious about email marketing, then advanced segmentation features are a must.

2. MESSAGE DESIGN AND SETUP

An email message that looks awful is unlikely to help your business. Design is a direct reflection of your brand and company, so every email message you send should accurately support your brand promise. People are very visual, and design is the first thing they see when they open your messages. Make sure you choose an email marketing tool that enables you to easily create professional-looking messages. The four factors you should focus on as you compare email marketing service providers are templates, customization, mobility, automation and campaign setup.

Templates

Are you a web or graphic designer? If not, creating email marketing messages that look great can be challenging. Fortunately, email marketing providers solve that problem by providing attractive templates that you can use to create your messages. You don't need to be a designer to use them. Most often, these templates are easy to manipulate using a drag-and-drop editing tool. You simply move the sections around, add new sections where you need them, add your text, upload images, and you're done. Look for an email marketing provider that offers a variety of templates as part of your subscription rather than as separate add-ons that you must pay for.

It's important to note that there are two schools of thought on message design for email marketing. Recent studies have found plain text messages that have not been highly designed but rather look like standard, personal email messages perform better than highly designed HTML email messages with lots of images and colors. In fact, ConvertKit, a popular email marketing tool, allows users to create and send only plain text messages. These types of statistics can vary from year to year and by the specific methodologies of the studies, so consider testing both types of designs to see what works best for your audience. Of course, to test both, your email marketing tool must provide both.

Customization

Templates are great, but sometimes you want even more customization for your email marketing messages. In that case, you need an email marketing tool that allows you to change all colors, move elements anywhere you want, add images and video in any way, and modify the code used to create your messages' designs to the tiniest detail. Not all email marketing tools give you access to the raw code that determines your messages' designs. If you'll need complete customization options now or in the future, do your research and pick a tool that provides it.

For advanced users, look for an email marketing tool that makes its application program interface (API) code available so your programmers can build and integrate exactly what you need when you need it. For example, if you want to automate a process but need your email marketing software to communicate with your internal project management software to do it, then your programmers would need access to your email marketing software's API to build that custom integration. Keep in mind, this is not something that most small businesses need, but if you're one of the companies that has a need for extensive customization, it could be important to you.

> **Definition**
> An *application program interface* (API) is computer code that enables two software programs to communicate with each other.

Mobility

Every day, more people open and read email messages on mobile devices, so it's essential that your email marketing messages display and function correctly on smartphones and tablets. In other words, mobile-friendliness shouldn't be an afterthought. It should be a priority. With that in mind, choose an email marketing provider that prioritizes mobile.

You need email templates that are automatically optimized for mobile devices. Templates should also be sized so they are viewable on both desktop and mobile devices (600 pixels wide is the optimal width). Images should be saved so they load quickly on all devices, and fonts should be readable on various devices.

Automation and Campaigns

Here's where email marketing really becomes powerful. Different email service providers use different terms to refer to individual email messages vs. sequences of email messages. For simplicity in this book, the terms "automation" and "campaign" will be used. *Email automations* are sequences of messages that are sent out based on actions that people take, such as submitting a form or clicking a link. Automations include simple email responders, such as the thank-you message sent after someone submits your subscription form. *Campaigns* are sent manually and include one message (since there are no messages sent automatically after the first).

For example, you might create an automation that goes out when someone requests your new free ebook. The first message could include the link to download the ebook. The second message could be scheduled to go out (i.e., "drip") two days later with useful tips, and a third message could go out three days after that with a discount on a product related to the ebook topic. On the other hand, you would send a campaign each time you send out your weekly newsletter. These are one-time messages with no follow-up messages or other automations attached to them.

Look for an email marketing provider that makes it easy for you to send one-time campaigns and automated sequences of messages. Many ESPs provide drag-and-drop tools to quickly set up automations, including what action triggers them to start, when messages should be sent, and even what messages people get depending on what they click within previous messages or other behaviors. You can get very advanced with automations, and as your email marketing program grows, you'll want to use these features. However, you need to choose a provider that offers them.

3. CONTENT AND DELIVERY

Once you've considered design features, you need to think about which email marketing tools allow you to create content that meets your goals as well as which provide the best deliverability rates. All email marketing tools make it easy to send messages to your contacts, but those messages aren't always optimized to ensure you get the best results.

Personalization and Dynamic Content

Personalization refers to more than just including a contact's name in the subject line and your message's greeting. In recent years, personalization has come to mean delivering highly personalized content based on each contact's behaviors and preferences. This type of changing content depends on the contact and is called dynamic content, adaptive content, or smart content. In simplest terms, the content in your messages changes depending on who is looking at it.

A great example of adaptive content is a retailer's recommendation tool. Have you ever looked at a product on a retailer's website and seen a bunch of suggested items on your screen that you might be interested in? Those suggestions change based on your behaviors, such as the search terms you've used and other items you've looked at. The content adapts to the visitor.

Dynamic content makes it possible to show offers to the right people at the right times. For example, if you send a holiday discount promotion to your subscribers, you can display dynamic content within your message showing people specific products they might want to use their discounts to purchase. Using the earlier pet supply store example, you could show dog-related products to people who have purchased similar items in the past and cat-related products to people who have purchased items for cats in the past. Rather than trying to please a large, broad audience, you can use smart rules within your email marketing application to show the best content to each person.

Dynamic content and personalization is getting increasingly popular, so even if you don't believe you'll use it soon, you might want to use it sooner than you think. With that in mind, be sure to include it as part of your overall comparison when you choose your email marketing tool.

Testing

Testing is an essential part of email marketing, so you should choose an email marketing provider that allows you to test as many elements of your campaigns and automations as possible. Many email marketing tools have built-in A/B split-testing functionality. With A/B testing, you can divide your audience into segments and show different messages to each segment. Ideally, you should only test one variable at a time.

For example, you could test your headline or the time of day when you send your message, but don't test both elements at the same time. The reason is simple. If you test multiple elements at the same time and see a significant lift in performance in one version of your message compared to the other, you won't know which element was responsible for the improvement in performance. Just as scientists test one variable at a time, so do email marketers.

Experimentation and testing are ongoing processes that you should be doing all the time. If your email marketing tool doesn't allow you to do adequate testing, then your performance will be limited. Therefore, do your due diligence and make sure that the provider you choose not only offers split testing but also makes it easy for you to perform split tests on all your campaigns and automations whenever you want.

Inbox Preview

Don't send email marketing messages without seeing how they'll first look in subscribers' inboxes. You can send test messages to yourself, but that takes multiple steps. If you have to send multiple tests, you could end up adding a lot of time to your email setup. Many email marketing tools include handy inbox preview features that allow you to see what your message will look like in recipients' inboxes with the click of a button.

Look for an email marketing tool that lets you see how your message will look in all of the most common email providers' inboxes, such as Gmail, Outlook, and Yahoo!. Also, look for a tool that lets you see how your message looks on desktops, smartphones, tablets, and multiple mobile operating systems. No matter how much time and effort you put into creating a great email message, all that time is wasted if what ends up in recipients' inboxes looks terrible or completely unreadable.

Deliverability

In Chapter 3, you learned about the importance of email deliverability and how to improve the deliverability of your messages, so review that chapter when you begin comparing email marketing tools. Ensure the one you select is focused on boosting deliverability rates. Not only should it follow all email delivery best practices, but consider choosing a tool that automatically takes care of some processes that can improve your message deliverability.

For example, some email marketing providers automatically stop sending messages to addresses that result in hard bounces or in soft bounces after a specific number of repeat soft bounces are detected. This type of automatic list cleansing happening behind the scenes saves you time and gives you peace of mind that bounces aren't negatively affecting the deliverability of your messages.

4. EMAIL MANAGEMENT

Some email marketing tools are so filled with features that they become difficult to use. Others are so simple that they might not offer the power you need. If you start to feel overwhelmed as you review email marketing options, go back to your goals and let them guide you. Don't overbuy, but make sure you have adequate functionality to leverage email marketing adequately. Following are several administration and management features you should think about as you compare email marketing tools.

Bulk Editing

How easy is it to edit multiple contacts in the email marketing tool? Do you have to manually open each contact record individually to make changes, or are there steps you can follow to edit many contacts at the same time? For example, if you want to add 100 contacts to a list or remove a tag from dozens of contacts, can you modify all 100 or dozens of records at the same time?

Businesses change, markets evolve, and your email marketing goals and strategy need to be flexible enough to grow with your business. If your email marketing tool can't keep up or requires hours of manual intervention to keep up, then it's not adequate. That's why it's so important to think about the future of your business and email marketing strategy when you choose an email marketing tool.

Integrations

Email marketing is so much more powerful when it is used in connection with your website, social media marketing, content marketing, online advertising, and other digital marketing tactics. You should choose an email marketing provider that integrates with the other tools you use to manage your marketing initiatives. When tools integrate, you reduce the amount of manual work that must be done to keep all your systems and programs synchronized.

At a minimum, your email marketing tool should integrate with Zapier (https:// zapier.com), a tool that connects web applications for streamlining and automating tasks. Many web-based applications integrate with Zapier as do most popular email marketing applications. You might also want to integrate your email marketing application with the tools you use for your invoicing, online calendar, ecommerce site, landing page, customer relationship management, online courses, customer service or online chat, help desk, and website analytics. The more integrations your email marketing provider offers, the more things you can automate to save time.

Customer Relationship Management (CRM)

Some email marketing tools also offer varying levels of CRM functionality (e.g., ActiveCampaign, ConvertKit, Infusionsoft, and Ontraport). If CRM is important to you, but you're not ready to invest in or don't need a full-blown CRM tool like Salesforce or SharpSpring, then one of these email marketing tools might fit your goals. An email marketing tool with CRM features makes it easy for you to follow contacts through your email marketing funnels, track all their interactions with your messages, and close deals with them.

Some email marketing tools with CRM functionality allow you to automate sales tasks and notifications, track sales activities, and qualify and score leads at different stages of the sales pipeline. It can get quite sophisticated, giving you the ability to capture, nurture, and close deals through customized sales processes and automations that you set up. Depending on the type of business you own and your sales and growth goals, choosing an email marketing tool that includes CRM features might make sense.

Performance Tracking and Reports

How do you know if your email marketing efforts are working if you can't track your results? You don't, which is why it's so important that your email marketing provider gives you access to easy-to-understand reports as well as the ability to download and manipulate your raw performance data. Even if you're not an analytics guru, you need to be able to quickly identify which messages are getting opened, which links are being clicked, and what needs to be improved.

In addition, choose an email marketing tool that integrates with Google Analytics or your preferred website analytics tool so you can track contact behaviors from your email messages to your website and vice versa. These behaviors are essential to helping you not only track performance but also develop campaigns and automations that deliver the most appropriate personalized, dynamic content. Remember, testing is an important part of email marketing success, and you need data and reports to determine which tests work and which don't.

5. ACCOUNT ADMINISTRATION AND HELP

As with all software, things will go wrong as you work with your email marketing tool. When you need help setting up your account, migrating from a different email marketing tool, or completing any other task within the application, it's important that support is available. Of course, this support and all the other features you need should be offered at a price you can afford.

Import/Export

When you start working with a new email marketing tool, you'll probably already have a list of customers you'll want to send messages to in the future. You might even already have a list of subscribers. If so, you need to feel confident that you can easily import those contacts into your new email marketing tool. You also need to know that once they're imported, they'll be added to the appropriate lists or the right tags will be appended to their contact records. This might also be important in the future if you acquire an offline list of opt-in subscribers at a conference or event. You don't want to have to enter every contact manually.

You may need to export your contacts at some point. For example, if you decide to switch to a different email marketing provider, you'll need to export your contacts in a format that you can then import into your new application. You never know what the future holds, so make sure you can export the list of contacts you own at any time. Don't worry: while the process to import or export contacts might differ from one email marketing tool to another, typically, step-by-step instructions are provided on screen.

Setup and Migration

Be careful when you evaluate email marketing providers that you research how to set up your new account and migrate your data from another provider. Some email marketing providers make the process simple and will even help you complete your migration at no additional charge. Others charge a hefty sum to set up your account and another fee to migrate your contacts and lists.

Keep in mind, migrating from one email marketing provider to another is never perfect. You will need to go into your campaigns, lists, and so on and make some tweaks. It's inevitable. However, you want to minimize the number of data adjustments, so look for a provider that makes migration easy. They should want your business, and it's in their best interest to help you migrate successfully so you remain a happy, paying customer. If the migration and setup processes are filled with obstacles, consider using another email marketing provider.

Support

Depending on your technical abilities, you might need a lot of ongoing help or just occasional help. At a minimum, you want to feel confident that you can get in touch with a knowledgeable person when something goes wrong or you can't figure out how to do something within your email marketing tool. Some email marketing providers offer support through an online knowledge base of text and video documents. Others offer phone, email, or chat support. Some offer all or a combination of these support options. Make sure the form of support you prefer is offered by the ESP you select.

Support hours and response times can also vary significantly. Some providers offer 24/7 support, while others offer support only during normal business hours Monday through Friday. Depending on your work hours, the times when support is available might be very important to you. In addition, some email marketing providers offer telephone support but only if you pay for a more expensive plan or pay for it as an add-on service. Be sure to check what forms of support are available as part of the subscription plan you select.

Pricing

Pricing can vary significantly between providers, so spend some time comparing how each email marketing provider charges users. Most email marketing providers charge users a monthly subscription fee based on four common pricing models: plan-based, subscriber-based, message-based, or freemium. Each of these pricing models is discussed in more detail in the remainder of this section.

> **Tip**
> Look for an email marketing provider that offers a free trial so you can do a test drive before you commit to paying.

Plan-Based Pricing Model

The plan-based pricing model sets monthly (or annual) fees for specific subscription plans. The cheapest plan includes the fewest features, and the most expensive plan includes the most features. It doesn't matter how many subscribers you have or how many email messages you send. You're always charged the same amount based on your chosen plan.

If you want to add more features, you need to switch to the plan that offers the features you want. Alternately, some email marketing providers offer some features as add-ons with individual fees for specific features so you can pick and choose which functionality you want to add to your account.

Subscriber-Based Pricing Model

The subscriber-based pricing model charges you for the number of contacts on your list.

> **Warning**
> Some email service providers using the subscriber-based pricing model with list-based subscriber management functionality count a contact multiple times if that contact appears on more than one list in your account. Keep this in mind as you compare pricing.

It doesn't matter how many messages you send to your contacts. All that matters is the number of contacts saved in your account. Typically, providers offer a tiered pricing structure that increases when you hit specific quantities of subscribers. For example, you could pay one fee if you have up to 500 contacts, a higher fee if you have 501 to 2,000 contacts, a higher fee if you have 2,001 to 5,000 contacts, and an even higher fee if you have 5,001 or more contacts.

Some email marketing providers use the subscriber-based pricing model in addition to plan-based pricing. If you choose an email marketing provider that charges users this way, you'd select your plan and your fee would be determined by the monthly plan fee in addition to any premium charged based on the number of contacts in your account.

Message-Based Pricing Model

The message-based pricing model charges fees to users based on the number of messages they send per month. It doesn't matter how many contacts are on your list. Instead, these providers count messages and bill you accordingly. If you have 100 contacts and send ten messages to all the contacts in your account during a single month, you'll be charged for 1,000 messages. If you have 1,000 contacts and you send them one message in a single month, you'll be charged the same thing—for 1,000 messages.

Similar to the subscriber-based pricing model, email marketing providers that use the message-based pricing model often set up tiers where the fee you're charged depends on the tier you're in each month. For example, the lowest tiered price might apply to users who send between 1 and 500 messages, and a higher fee would apply to users who send between 501 and 1,000 messages. Also similar to the subscriber-based pricing model, some email marketing providers combine the message-based pricing model with the plan-based pricing model.

Freemium Pricing Model

While uncommon, some email marketing providers use a freemium pricing model where the tier with the fewest features or that allows the fewest subscribers or sent messages per month is offered for free. Once you exceed the limits of the free tier, you're required to pay to continue using the application. At that point, you would be charged based on the plan you choose, the number of contacts in your account, the number of messages you send, or a combination of these pricing models.

The freemium pricing model is very popular for SaaS tools because it allows people to try an application and get committed to it enough that changing to another tool would be too inconvenient and time-consuming. It's very effective for companies, so be careful. It can be tempting to use the tool that is offered for free, but it might not be the best one for you in the long term. As you learned earlier in this chapter, switching from one email marketing provider to another can be done, but it's rarely problem-free. Choose the right tool to meet your goals, and that might not be the cheapest (or free) one.

MAKING YOUR FINAL DECISION

Narrow the list of email marketing tools that might work well for you down to three, and then compare them side-by-side using each of the factors discussed in this chapter. Think long-term, but don't overbuy. You want a tool that gives you flexibility and room to grow, but you don't want to be overwhelmed and overpay for features you'll never use. Make a list and compare the pros and cons of each tool. It's very likely that one will come out on top.

Chapter 5

Types of Email Marketing Funnels

I t's important that you choose an email marketing tool that enables you to build automated sequences. These automations are created when you set up processes to send messages to people on your list once and let them run on an ongoing basis without your intervention aside from monitoring their performance. If you can't build automated sequences of messages, then you can't build email marketing funnels that push consumers through your overarching strategic marketing funnel, which you learned about in Chapter 2. Your email marketing results will be limited if you cannot engage consumers at each stage of the marketing funnel.

To effectively move people through your overarching strategic marketing funnel, you need to build specific email marketing funnels. These email marketing funnels are created to bring prospective customers into your overall marketing funnel and keep important prospects from falling out over time. Your email marketing funnels can be simple or complex depending on their purpose, but they're all triggered by specific actions that flag a person as someone who could be pushed further through the overall marketing funnel if they received some additional prodding via an email message.

SELECTING AN EMAIL MARKETING FUNNEL

You can create dozens and dozens of email marketing funnel campaigns to move consumers through your overall marketing funnel. In fact, you're limited only by your creativity. However, all email marketing funnels fall into one of three categories: acquire, nurture, or convert.

The type of email marketing funnel you create depends on your goals for it. Is your list small? Do you need to collect more leads at the top of the marketing funnel? If so, you need an acquisition funnel. Do you need to keep leads in the middle of the marketing funnel engaged so they'll move to the bottom of the funnel? Then you need a nurturing funnel. Have you identified customers who are at the bottom of the marketing funnel and only need an additional nudge to make a purchase? A conversion funnel is the answer. Use Figure 5–1 on page 61 to identify where your audience is in the marketing funnel, what your goals are, and which type of email funnel you need to create to reach those goals for each audience.

Acquisition Email Marketing Funnels

Acquisition funnels serve a very specific purpose. They attract leads to your subscriber list so you can market to them in the future. When you create an acquisition funnel, you need to make sure you're attracting the right kind of leads. With that in mind, your acquisition tactics should appeal to your target audience. They must be relevant, meaningful, and useful to your target audience, or you're wasting your time and money by building a list of leads that will never convert into sales.

Acquisition funnels should start with a low-risk offer. Often, leads won't be familiar with your brand, products, or services. You need to offer them something of equal or greater value based on their perception of the worth of their email addresses. Don't

MATCHING MARKETING FUNNELS TO YOUR GOALS

There are three types of email marketing funnels based on your goals:

1. To acquire prospective customer leads

2. To nurture prospective customer leads over time

3. To convert prospective customer leads into buying customers or to take another specific, desired action

Audience Marketing Funnel Position	Your Goal	Email Funnel to Use
Top	You have a small list and need to generate more leads to fill the top of the funnel.	Acquisition
Middle	You need to keep the people who are on your list and in the middle of the funnel engaged so they move to the bottom of the funnel.	Nurture
Bottom	You need to nudge people who are at the bottom of the funnel to act so you can reach a specific marketing or business objective.	Conversion

FIGURE 5–1. Email Marketing Funnel Matrix

expect leads to make a purchase immediately. That isn't the purpose of an acquisition funnel. Your goal is to acquire as many relevant email addresses as possible so you can market to them and move them from the top of the funnel (where they are now) to the middle of the funnel and, finally, to the bottom of the funnel where they make a purchase and, hopefully, become loyal customers and brand advocates.

Think of it this way: if you walked up to someone at a business networking event whom you've never met before, would you start the conversation by saying, "Hi, do you want to buy my widgets?" You need to warm up your leads before you can try to sell anything to them. The same is true in email marketing. Warm up your leads by giving them useful, interesting, and relevant content and information before you try to sell anything to them. If you start with a hard sales message, your list of leads won't grow much, but if you start with meaningful information and build a relationship before you go for the hard sell, your list will grow faster and your conversions will be higher.

You'll learn more about growing your email list and using lead magnets to attract appropriate leads in Chapters 6 and 7. For now, it's important to learn about some of the most common acquisition email marketing funnels that have been proven to successfully boost subscriber lists.

> **Tip**
> The goal of an acquisition email marketing funnel is quantity. You want to fill your overall marketing funnel with as many relevant customer prospect leads as possible.

Lead Magnets

Lead magnets are free content that you offer to your target audience in exchange for their email addresses. You could create ebooks, reports, checklists, infographics, worksheets, or tutorials and use each as a lead magnet to motivate leads to give you their email addresses in exchange for a free download of the content. If a person shows interest in your lead magnet, then you can assume they're interested in your industry and the types of products or services you offer. That means you have a good chance of moving them through the overall marketing funnel over time. This is why creating relevant lead magnets is critical to your email marketing success.

Live Webinars

Live webinars can be used for lead acquisition and lead nurturing. Why are live webinars especially useful? It's because there is more of a commitment to attend a live webinar than there is to download a free lead magnet. Subscribers sign up for a date to "attend," thus putting you and your company front and center in their inbox and calendar. If you can provide extremely valuable information in a webinar that people are likely to want even if they've never heard of your brand before, you might have success using live webinars for lead acquisition. It's all about value, so you need to make sure your webinar exceeds the time investment and the perceived value of each lead's personal information and email addresses.

Nurturing Email Marketing Funnels

Nurturing funnels are used to keep the right people in your overall marketing funnel over time and actively move them to the bottom of the overall marketing funnel where they make a purchase. The truth is not everyone is ready to make a purchase when you acquire them on your email marketing list. Depending on the type of business you operate, people's needs, and consumers' positions on the buyer journey, it could take days, weeks, or months to move them from prospect to conversion. That's why nurturing your leads through email marketing is so important.

Lead-nurturing email marketing funnels also help you keep important people from falling out of your marketing funnel and allows you to remove leads that will never reach the bottom to make a purchase. You don't want to waste your time or money promoting your business to leads that will never turn into buying customers. Instead, you want to spend your time and money nurturing leads who you can build relationships with so when the time comes to make a purchase (which you can often speed up using nurturing messages), they choose your company.

Again, lead nurturing is about building relationships with prospective, current, and prior customers. Messages build trust between leads and your brand. They might remove obstacles that are keeping people from moving to the bottom of your overall marketing funnel, and they keep your brand top-of-mind over time. Here are some popular nurturing funnels you can create to move consumers toward the bottom of your marketing funnel.

Welcome

When someone subscribes to your list, send them a series of messages in a welcome nurturing funnel. The first message simply welcomes them. The second provides links to additional resources on your website or blog, and the third introduces what you do and offer.

Free Trial

Offer a free trial on your website to give interested leads a closer look at what your product does. Once someone signs up for the free trial, send a series of email messages to ensure the trial is going well, offer tips to use your product, provide sources to get answers to questions, and finally, tell recipients that the free trial is expiring and how to make a purchase to continue using your product.

Anniversary Funnel

On the anniversary date when someone joined your list, made a specific purchase, or took another noteworthy action, send your anniversary nurturing funnel. The first message thanks them for taking that earlier action. The second message reminds them of some of the benefits they get from their relationship with you, and the third message provides links to some products chosen specifically for them based on their prior purchases and behaviors.

Survey

People love to give their opinions, so they're likely to respond to surveys that you send to them if those surveys are relevant and don't take too long to complete. A great way to re-engage your subscribers to ensure you're sending them the most useful content and to let them know their opinions matter to you is to send them a survey.

Start with a message that warns them the survey is coming and asking them to be on the lookout for it. Make sure you explain why you're conducting the survey, what you'll do with the information, and how long the survey will take to complete. Your second message should include the survey. You can survey your existing list for free using a tool like Google Forms (www.google.com/forms/about). If you need a more robust survey tool, you can try SurveyMonkey (www.surveymonkey.com) or QuestionPro (www.questionpro.com).

Top-of-Mind

Sending useful content is a great way to keep your brand at the top of your subscribers' minds. This is particularly important if you have a long sales cycle or you sell seasonal products. With a top-of-mind funnel, you create a series of messages that are sent at specific times of year or when subscribers take specific actions, such as visiting a page on your website or clicking a link in your email newsletter. Each message includes a quick tip, a how-to article, or another piece of content that helps them solve a problem related to your product or service. The last message promotes that product or service.

Unsubscribe

What do you do when someone unsubscribes from your list? Do you let them get away, or do you try to keep them by sending messages in an unsubscribe nurturing funnel? Before you let anyone unsubscribe from your list, you should try to keep them. Send a message that asks them if they're sure they want to unsubscribe. Provide reasons why they shouldn't, and if your email marketing service provider allows it, give them the option to unsubscribe only from specific types of messages. For example, they might want to unsubscribe from promotional messages, but they want to continue getting your newsletter with educational content.

Webinars

Webinars can be used to acquire leads (as mentioned earlier), but they also work well to move people from the top of the funnel to the middle, and even from the middle of the funnel to the bottom. For example, once you've acquired leads with a specific lead magnet, you could hold a webinar that provides the next logical step that people should take after reading, viewing, or using the lead magnet. This type of webinar moves them to the middle of the funnel. From there, you could offer a discount on your related service or product to move them to the bottom of the funnel. Webinar funnel messages vary depending on how you're using them to move people through your overall marketing funnel.

Subscriber Re-engagement

Over time, some of the contacts on your subscriber list will stop opening your messages. It makes no sense to continue emailing people who have no interest in your products and services. In addition, emailing people who don't interact with your messages can damage the overall deliverability of your messages, as you learned in Chapter 3. Therefore, it's important to identify unengaged contacts and try to re-engage them. To do this, create a subscriber re-engagement nurturing funnel where you mention that you haven't heard from subscribers in a while and remind them about the great content you've been sharing. Next, ask them if they want to continue getting messages from you. If so, they need to click a link to stay subscribed. This is the easiest way to determine who wants to stay engaged with your brand.

Conversion Email Marketing Funnels

Conversion email marketing funnels are created to motivate recipients to make a purchase or complete another action right now. In this book, the focus is on using conversion email marketing funnels to generate sales. Often, conversion email marketing funnels are used with other sales support tasks, such as phone calls because these messages are sent to people who are at the bottom of the marketing funnel and ready to buy.

Sending highly targeted, personalized messages is essential to your success when it comes to conversion email marketing funnels. Make sure the actions you want recipients to take are extremely relevant and specific. In other words, the call to action should be abundantly clear. Some popular conversion email marketing funnels are introduced in the remainder of this section. Be sure to read Chapter 8 to learn more details about developing an email marketing conversion funnel.

Abandoned Cart

When someone starts the checkout process on your website but doesn't complete their purchase, don't let them get away. You should immediately follow up with an abandoned cart funnel that sends a series of messages created to motivate them to complete their purchase. The first message might say something as simple as, "Did you forget to complete your purchase?" The second message could offer a discount or free shipping, and a third message could capitalize on the recipient's fear of missing out if they don't make the purchase.

Trial Upgrade

If you offer a free trial of your product to acquire leads or move people to the middle of your marketing funnel but they don't purchase your product after the trial ends, you should follow up with a trial upgrade conversion funnel. The messages in this series should remind them of the benefits they'll miss out on if they don't upgrade. Be sure to offer ways for them to get more help. It's also effective to send a message in this sequence that offers free setup, free training, or a discount on the product price.

Free Demonstration

Free demos are often offered for complex products, particularly software-as-a-service (SaaS) products that people need to see in action to truly understand. Not only do people have to give up their contact information and email addresses to get a free demo, but they also need to speak with a salesperson. This is not a low-risk proposition for people, so free demos are usually used to move leads from the middle of the funnel to the bottom or to motivate people at the bottom to finally make a purchase.

When someone signs up for a free demo, you must make them feel comfortable with that decision. Send a series of messages that confirms the demo time and explains what will be discussed. Follow up with a reminder message before the demo, and after the demo, send additional messages with useful information, helpful links, testimonials, case studies, and other content that will remove any barriers to buying.

Cross-Sell and Add-Ons

The perfect time to present complementary products to a customer is when they're actively making a purchase on your website. However, don't forget to offer complementary products as soon as the transaction is completed. You can create cross-sell and add-on conversion funnels that are sent as soon as customers purchase specific products or services. Your messages should introduce the products, explain why they're perfect complements to the original purchase, and include customer reviews. You can even include a discount on the complementary products to boost sales.

Special Offers and Promotions

Often, consumers want to make a purchase but need one more nudge to take action. This is particularly true since people are so busy these days. It's easy to put off making a purchase until that purchase is no longer important or necessary. To give people on your list that extra nudge, create special offer and promotion conversion funnels that are sent when people view specific pages on your website or on specific dates for seasonal or time-sensitive products. Send a message hyping the discount or promotion, and follow-up with additional messages reminding people when the offer ends and why they don't want to miss out on getting the products they're interested in through the special offer. Including a countdown timer in these messages works extremely well to increase the response rate.

Refer a Friend

All your subscribers are connected to other people online and offline, which means your brand has the potential to reach far and wide if you create refer-a-friend programs and promote them through email marketing funnels. These funnels can be triggered after someone on your list makes a purchase or any other time you choose. Your messages should explain how the program works and what people get for referring a friend. Make sure they can share it online and offline. To turn this into a conversion funnel, offer a special discount to recipients who actually refer friends.

Loyalty Programs

Earlier in this chapter, you learned about using anniversary funnels to nurture subscribers. You can take that concept a step further and create loyalty programs that reward your most loyal customers. Create a funnel that is triggered to start based on a subscriber's actions (for example, the subscriber makes a purchase for the first, second, third, or any number of times you choose). Messages in this funnel should explain how the loyalty program works and make the customer feel special as a member of this exclusive group.

Keep in mind, loyal customers can become your most vocal brand advocates, so be sure to nurture them using personalized, dynamic content. Offer a discount when recipients join the program to turn this into a conversion funnel that leads to a purchase right now. You'll learn more about how to do this in Chapter 9.

Remove Obstacles to Purchase

A key part of leveraging the power of conversion email funnels is removing obstacles to purchases. These obstacles vary greatly depending on your industry and between your customer segments. Typically, removing obstacles requires an email marketing funnel coupled with a sales call. Your email marketing funnel could provide a case study that explains how another customer overcame the same obstacle. Follow-up messages should offer more helpful information and additional testimonials.

HOW TO BUILD AN EMAIL MARKETING FUNNEL

Building an email marketing funnel isn't difficult, but it requires some planning, the right tools, a bit of technical knowledge (or access to someone who has technical skills), and some time. Once you've selected your email marketing tool, you'll need to review their tutorial videos or help articles to learn the specific steps that tool requires to create your funnel. Each tool is different, and the steps change often as software is updated, so go directly to the source (your tool's help documentation or support team) to learn the correct steps.

As a general overview, let's assume you're building a lead magnet email marketing funnel to acquire new leads for your list. The first step you need to do is create a form within your email marketing tool where people can enter their email addresses to download the lead magnet. You'll also need to determine where people who submit this form will "live" in your email marketing contact database. That means you need to identify a list that they will be added to when they submit the form. In addition, you might be able to add tags to further describe them (depending on whether your email marketing tool offers a tagging feature), which is important if you use subscriber-based contact management as discussed in Chapter 4.

Once your form and list are created, you can build your email automation sequence. This includes identifying each of the triggers that cause the messages in your sequence to be sent as well as the content of each message. For example, you might create a sequence that sends a message with the lead magnet download link as soon as the form is submitted. Next, you could set up your sequence so a follow-up message is sent out two days later. After that, you might decide to send another message a few days later or to send one message to people who clicked the link in your message to download the lead magnet and another message to people who haven't clicked the link within 24 hours.

You can create your automated sequence of messages however you want, but once that sequence is built, you need to activate it (so it's live and working) and double-check that it's connected to the form you created to trigger it. Once you know everything is set up correctly in your email marketing tool, it's time to add the form to your website or landing page so people can see and use it. The steps to embed the form typically require that you copy some code from your email marketing tool and paste it into your website's code. Many email marketing providers offer free plug-ins that integrate directly with WordPress and other website and landing page building tools, so it's very easy to add your form to your site.

Once the form has been added, publish your web page and test it. If everything works, you can start promoting it through social media, online advertising, and so on. You need to get traffic to the page, or no one will know about your lead magnet or submit the form to subscribe to your list. You'll learn more about using opt-in forms and acquiring email addresses in Chapter 6, but this overview gives you a basic introduction to how the process of building email marketing funnels works. Thanks to email marketing tools and website and landing page builders, it's quite easy. Once you build your first funnel, you won't feel intimidated by the process anymore.

Creating Your Own Email Marketing Funnels

There are so many email marketing funnels you can create to acquire leads at the top of your marketing funnel, build relationships with leads in the middle, and convert those leads into sales at the bottom. Check out Chapter 13 for examples that you can use for your own business.

Chapter 6

Growing Your List

Email marketing doesn't work unless you build a list of people to send messages to who are interested in your products or services. If you've captured email addresses from your prior customers, then you have a great head start. Every person who has purchased from you in the past could become a repeat customer. Email marketing helps to strengthen their relationship with your brand, so in time, they could become loyal customers.

Now that you have read about the general concepts behind funnels, tools, and how to make sure your messages have a chance to get delivered, you can dig into the task of growing your list. As you learned in Chapter 5, nurturing your brand's relationship with current and past customers is critical to your business, but you need to invest time and money into connecting with new prospects. If you're not continually adding more leads to the top of your overall marketing funnel, your business growth will be limited. You need to cast a wide net, then use email, content, and sales tactics to push those leads through the marketing funnel until they make a purchase. According to Ascend2's 2017 "Email List Growth Trends Survey Summary Report," the most effective tactics to grow your email list according to marketers are social media advertising, content marketing, and search engine optimization. Using these tactics and more to build your list is vital to growing your business. Remember, the power is in your list. You own it, and you can use it to your advantage.

There are five key steps to growing your email list:

1. Develop relevant opt-in offers.
2. Create effective online opt-in forms.
3. Drive targeted visitors to your online opt-in forms.
4. Show your offer to those visitors.
5. Improve the results of your online opt-in forms.

This chapter walks you through all five of these critical steps so you have the necessary foundation to grow an email opt-in list of subscribers who want to hear from your brand and have the potential to move further through your marketing funnel with effective email engagement and offers.

STEP 1: DEVELOP RELEVANT OPT-IN OFFERS

The first step to growing your email marketing list is to develop an offer with a high enough perceived value that your target audience is willing to provide their email addresses in exchange for it. Your offer could be an amazing weekly newsletter, a discount on a future purchase, a free trial or demonstration of your product, or a free tangible item, which marketers refer to as an incentive or lead magnet. In other words, it's an item that the target audience of prospects is so interested in that it attracts them to your subscription form like a magnet and motivates them to submit the form to join your list.

> **Tip**
> The terms *opt-in form* and *subscription form* are often used interchangeably to refer to the form used to add people to your email list. In simplest terms, people use the form to opt-in or subscribe to your email list.

You can learn about creating lead magnets in detail in Chapter 7. For now, think of offers as the bait that will attract people through all the ways you promote it, including advertising, search engine optimization, guest blog posting, and so on. These are the tactics you'll use in step three of the list-building process discussed in this chapter. If your offer isn't valuable enough to your target audience, it doesn't matter how much you promote it online and offline—no one will be interested enough to take action. That means not only won't you get traffic to your online opt-in form, but you also won't get any subscribers.

With that said, an opt-in form that doesn't promise a special offer or free content as a lead magnet could simply promote all the great content you'll share in your email newsletter. For example, your opt-in form could simply say, "Sign up now so you don't miss the important news and tips you need to be successful." You can get more specific with your promise with copy that says, "Subscribe now and get a critical tip to grow your

FIGURE 6–1. Simple Opt-In Form without a Lead Magnet Offer

business every week delivered directly to your inbox." You'll learn more about writing your opt-in form copy in step two, but these examples demonstrate that you don't have to give anything more away than the promise of useful and meaningful information to motivate people to subscribe to your email marketing list. You can see a simple opt-in form like this created using ActiveCampaign in Figure 6–1.

STEP 2: CREATE EFFECTIVE ONLINE OPT-IN FORMS

You can create opt-in forms directly in most email marketing tools, such as ActiveCampaign, MailChimp, and Constant Contact. Simply follow the directions within your email marketing software to create the form, copy the form code, and paste it into your website. It's a very simple process, but there is usually a problem. Most opt-in form designs offered within email marketing tools are very basic. You might be limited by the layout, colors, and even the amount or placement of copy. If you're serious about growing your email marketing list, you should consider using a more robust opt-in form tool.

Choosing an Opt-In Form Tool

There are a variety of applications you can use to create beautifully designed opt-in forms that can be displayed in a variety of places on your website. Most of these tools offer libraries of free opt-in form templates complete with images, fonts, and colors chosen by experienced designers. Often, these templates have been tested and have proved to convert visitors to subscribers so you can feel confident using them.

Here is a list of several opt-in form tools you can choose from if you want a better design than what your email marketing tool provides:

- *OptinMonster* (http://optinmonster.com): OptinMonster was developed to do one thing, and the tool does it very well—create and track the performance of opt-in forms. A wide variety of opt-in form styles and functionalities are available to choose from.
- *Sumo* (https://sumo.com): Sumo offers several opt-in form tools to display forms in different areas of your website, as well as a social media-sharing button tool.
- *Unbounce* (https://unbounce.com): Unbounce offers tools to create landing pages and opt-in forms (called "convertables").
- *Leadpages* (www.leadpages.net): Leadpages offers landing page design and opt-in form pop-ups (called "Leadboxes").
- *Instapage* (https://instapage.com): Instapage offers landing page design and opt-in form creation tools.
- *MailMunch* (www.mailmunch.co): MailMunch offers a variety of opt-in form features to display different kinds of forms on your site.
- *Thrive Themes* (https://thrivethemes.com): ThriveThemes is a WordPress plugin that offers landing page and opt-in form creation.

Each of the preceding tools gives you the ability to make beautiful opt-in forms. For example, the form in Figure 6–2 (on page 73) was created using OptinMonster and looks much better than the basic form shown in Figure 6–1.

Many opt-in form tools include free trials or free accounts with basic functionality. Prices and features change often, so visit each website to review the current offerings. Be very careful to make sure the tool and plan you choose allows you to capture leads from all your monthly traffic. Some limit the amount of traffic or form submissions allowed at different price points. If your form looks great but isn't displayed to some of your visitors, then don't use it.

Furthermore, some opt-in form tools don't integrate directly with all email marketing tools. In other words, you can't log into your opt-in form tool, enter some information from your email marketing tool (usually a license key), click a button, and automatically add or edit contacts in your email marketing contact list based on how they interact with your opt-in forms. That means you'll either need to use another tool, such as Zapier, to integrate the two tools or you'll need to manually add or edit leads that come from your great-looking opt-in forms to your email marketing contact list. The purpose of using these tools is to streamline processes by automating

FIGURE 6–2. Opt-In Form Created with OptinMonster

them. Therefore, don't use an opt-in form tool that doesn't integrate with your email marketing tool.

Writing Your Opt-In Form Copy

Once you've decided which tool you're going to use to create your opt-in forms, it's time to write the copy for the form. It's essential that the form copy excites your target audience and compels them to take action. They need to understand the value they'll get when they give you their email addresses, and they need to feel confident doing so. To that end, following are seven things you should try to accomplish in your copy.

1. Answer the Question, "What's in It for Me?"

An essential question that every marketing message should answer for consumers is, "What's in it for me?" Copywriters use the acronym WIIFM to refer to this critical question. Your copy must explain the benefits your audience will get when they submit your opt-in form.

For example, if you're not offering a lead magnet but, rather, simply inviting people to join your weekly newsletter list, what benefit do they get from subscribing? Instead of using copy that says, "Subscribe to my newsletter," a fitness coach could use copy that says, "Subscribe now and get my weekly exercise video to keep the weight off."

2. Describe the Offer

You must explain what people will get when they submit your opt-in form, or many of your website visitors won't feel confident entering their email addresses. Remember, they have to feel like what you're giving them is worth more than their email addresses. No one wants an inbox cluttered with spam or useless messages. People are extremely protective of their inboxes, so be very clear in what you're offering. In the fitness coach example above, the coach could have offered weekly exercise tips, but instead, the copy is extremely clear about what the coach is offering to subscribers—a weekly *video* with exercise tips.

3. Set Expectations

To boost confidence, it's important to set clear expectations for what happens next when someone submits your opt-in form. The first step is to explain how often they'll hear from you. Will you email them weekly or monthly? Will you send occasional promotional messages? Again, refer to the previous fitness coach example and notice how the copy says subscribers will receive weekly messages. Leads know exactly what they'll get and when they'll get it when they submit the opt-in form. If the fitness coach plans to send additional promotional messages that are separate from the weekly video messages, they could add a phrase to the copy that says, "And occasional promotional messages announcing cool new products and offers."

4. Build Trust

Many people who you're trying to capture through your opt-in form won't be familiar with your brand or will only vaguely recognize it. They might not be familiar with your reputation, so it's important to build trust with them immediately. They need to believe that you'll deliver on what you're promising in your opt-in form. To that end, add some proof to your opt-in form to support your claims.

For example, mention how many other people already subscribe in your opt-in form copy, saying something like, "Join 10,000 of your peers," or "Join 10,000 people just like you," or "Join 10,000 like-minded people." If your target audience is made up of a specific segment of people, address them specifically in your copy. For example, a fitness coach whose clientele is made up of elite athletes could write: "Join 10,000 other high-performance athletes." Adding this copy taps into people's fear of missing out (FOMO). Subconsciously, they'll think that if so many other people like them are already subscribing to your email list, they should as well, or they might miss something important.

In addition, it's a good idea to include copy on your opt-in form that gives people confidence that your form is secure and you won't share their email addresses. Copy as simple as "We promise we won't spam you or share your email address with anyone else" works well. This adds another level of peace of mind that can make a difference in how well your form converts visitors into subscribers.

Finally, if your form has enough room, include one or more testimonials. You don't even have to write additional copy to precede a testimonial if it's specifically related to your opt-in offer. For example, if you're a fitness coach offering a free ebook and you have a testimonial from a subscriber saying they lost ten pounds after using the tips in that ebook, display it on your opt-in form. No additional copy is needed because the testimonial is so relevant and specific. For less relevant or specific testimonials, you could include copy before the testimonials that says, "Here's what other subscribers are saying about us." Of course, if a testimonial is too irrelevant and won't help convert visitors into subscribers through a specific form, don't include it. Instead, display less relevant testimonials on your website or another opt-in form where they'll be more useful.

5. Include a Powerful Call to Action

Your opt-in form should have a specific call to action, which is often referred to by its acronym, CTA. What is the one thing you want people to do after they see your opt-in form? Most likely, you want them to enter their email addresses and click a button to be added to your email marketing list. Therefore, make it extremely clear how to complete that action on your form. Use a large and obvious call to action button in a color that contrasts with the rest of your form's color palette so it's easy to see. There should be no question what a visitor should do next after viewing your opt-in form.

The copy for your call to action should be extremely action-oriented. Include that copy on the button that people click to submit your opt-in form. That means the button on your form shouldn't just say "submit." That's not good enough to maximize submissions. Instead, your button copy should describe a specific action, use first-person pronouns (e.g., I, me, my, mine), and create a sense of urgency whenever possible.

For example, if you're simply offering a subscription to your weekly newsletter, use copy that says, "Sign me up now," or "I want my weekly tips." On the other hand, if you're offering an ebook as a lead magnet, use copy that says, "Send me my ebook now," or "Get my ebook now." Some opt-in form tools even allow you to include countdown timers in your forms for limited time offers. These are great for creating a sense of urgency, particularly when you're offering a lead magnet like a live webinar or a promotional contest that has a specific end date.

6. Integrate Your Opt-In Form Copy with the Design

Your opt-in form copy doesn't have to include every one of these elements. Many opt-in forms are small, and you don't have a lot of room for copy. Usually, the simpler your opt-in forms are, the better. However, if you work with an experienced copywriter, they will be able to communicate a lot of this information in very few words. It's an art, and not every writer can do it well.

Also, consider how much information you're trying to collect from leads through your opt-in form. The more fields you include and the more information you try to collect, the lower your conversion rates will be and the less room you'll have for powerful messages to attract and convert visitors into subscribers. Yes, it's nice to have people's titles and company names, but is that information truly necessary for your future marketing programs to work? Limit your forms to as few fields as possible, and your results will improve. You saw an example of a simple opt-in form with just one field in Figure 6–2. Look at Figure 6–2A to see an example of an opt-in form that includes many fields.

FIGURE 6–2A. Opt-In Form with Many Fields

7. Write Beyond the Opt-In Form

Your copywriting doesn't end with the opt-in form. What happens when someone submits that form? Will they be taken to a page on your website that thanks them for subscribing? You need to write that, too. In addition, you should follow up with an email message that thanks them for subscribing and welcomes them to your community. If your opt-in offer promised a tangible incentive, such as an ebook or white paper, you need to deliver it via email.

Next, think beyond the opt-in welcome message. If you send a weekly email newsletter to all your list subscribers, then you know they'll hear from you again soon after they receive your welcome message. However, if you don't send a newsletter often (or at all), it's important that you create an email automation with a sequence of messages so you can continue to build a relationship with every subscriber. You'll learn more about writing email messages like these in Chapter 10.

STEP 3: DRIVE TARGETED VISITORS TO YOUR ONLINE OPT-IN FORMS

Your target audience needs to see your opt-in forms, or you won't be able to grow your email marketing list effectively. It doesn't help to have a list filled with people who will never buy from you. Fortunately, there are many steps you can take to bring the audience you want to connect with to your website where they'll see your opt-in forms.

Here we'll focus on three strategies you can use to drive more qualified traffic to your opt-in forms. Keep in mind, this list isn't exhaustive, but it gives you a great starting point to start building your email marketing list.

BUILDING YOUR EMAIL MARKETING LIST OFFLINE

While this book focuses primarily on digital marketing activities, don't forget to build your email marketing list offline, too. You can do this using sign-up forms in your brick-and-mortar location or at conferences and trade shows. It's also important to use offline initiatives to send people to your online opt-in forms where they can subscribe to your list. For example, include the URL for your opt-in form (assuming you have it available on a specific page on your website) on your business cards, print ads, point-of-sale signage, brochures, and so on. Lead magnets work particularly well at driving offline leads to your online opt-in forms.

Lead Magnets

Lead magnets are incentives used to encourage people to submit your opt-in form. They could be ebooks, white papers, checklists, worksheets, templates, tools, or any other valuable piece of content that your target audience would want to solve a problem or learn useful information. They could even be promotional offers, such as a discount or free trial. A lead magnet can be promoted as a stand-alone incentive through advertising, social media marketing, and other marketing tactics. Lead magnets are discussed in detail in Chapter 7.

Third-Party Content

Third-party content includes content you publish on other websites to drive traffic back to your own opt-in form. One of the most effective types of third-party content is guest blog posts. Many popular blogs allow you to submit guest posts for free. Do a Google search for "submit a guest post" or a similar keyword phrase to find blogs your target audience might read that accept guest posts. Visit the blog and look for guest post submission guidelines. Be sure to follow these guidelines exactly to increase your chances of getting your posts published.

Every piece of content you publish on another website creates a new entry point to your site. Make sure you include a link back to the page with your opt-in form on it either within your post or in your author biography that is published with your post. The key is to find sites where your audience already spends time so you're sending qualified leads from your guest posts to your opt-in form.

The same is true of other types of third-party content. Don't be afraid to seek creative ways to drive traffic to your opt-in forms. For example, visit online forums, Facebook Groups, and LinkedIn Groups where your target audience is likely to spend time, and look for people who ask questions related to your lead magnet or your products and services. Join the conversation and include a link to your opt-in form for more information. You can do the same thing on popular question-and-answer sites like Quora.com. But don't self-promote in your responses. Instead, answer the question in detail and offer the link to your opt-in form simply as a way for people to get more information.

Social Media

Social media marketing is an excellent way to drive traffic to your website and your opt-in forms. Post useful information to your social media accounts with links to your opt-in forms. Lead magnets work extremely well to build your list using social media marketing tactics. You can share sneak peaks from the lead magnet, images, charts, related videos, and more to boost interest in your lead magnet and motivate people to click the link and submit your opt-in form. Any social media posts that lead to your opt-in form should be pinned to the top of your newsfeed if possible. You can do this in Facebook, Twitter, Pinterest, and other popular social media tools so people are sure to see your opt-in post before they see other posts from you.

You can also use social media to promote creative lead magnets, such as social media contests and giveaways. Host a contest on Facebook, Instagram, Twitter, and so on using tools like ShortStack (www.shortstack.com), Woobox (https://woobox.com), or Wishpond (www.wishpond.com) to set it up. To make this work for list-building purposes, people should be required to provide an email address to enter the contest. Just make sure the prize is of equal or lesser perceived value than an email address, or no one will enter the contest.

Advertising

Online advertising on targeted websites or through Google AdWords, Facebook ads, Twitter ads, LinkedIn ads, and other digital advertising services can work extremely well to increase opt-in form submissions, particularly if you're offering a lead magnet that your target audience really wants. Of course, great copywriting also matters, but if you don't have a great lead magnet to advertise, your conversions will probably be lower than they could be.

The key to success is to choose laser-focused audiences to show your ads to. Many email marketers working in a wide variety of industries have great success in building their lists by advertising lead magnets through promoted posts on Facebook. The targeting tools are excellent and allow you to hone in on very specific people. Make sure you use a compelling image, in addition to powerful copywriting, and you should see your opt-ins climb.

In addition to traditional digital advertising, test native advertising (also referred to as sponsored posts or paid posts), where you pay a website or blog to publish a post for you with a link back to your opt-in form page. Just make sure the website or blog discloses that the post has been paid for, or you could violate the Federal Code of Regulations' rules related to disclosing material connections in online content.

Retargeting is another great way to convert visitors to subscribers. In simplest terms, retargeting ads are shown to people who already visited specific pages on your website or displayed specific behaviors while engaging with your content. If you set up retargeting using a tool like Google AdWords, people will be shown your ad on other sites after they leave your site. If you set up retargeting using a tool like Facebook Ads, they'll be shown your ads when they visit Facebook after leaving your site or displaying your chosen trigger behaviors. For example, if someone sees your opt-in form on a page of your website, then leaves your site, if you set up a retargeting campaign to be triggered by that action, the visitor should see one of your ads on another site after they leave yours.

The purpose of retargeting is to show the same offer to a targeted audience repeatedly so the fear of missing out is piqued, interest increases, and more people take the next step to submit the form. It's extremely effective simply because often people just need an extra reminder or gentle nudge before they act.

STEP 4: SHOW YOUR OFFER TO YOUR VISITORS

Once you've driven traffic to your website, make sure visitors see your opt-in forms. There are dozens and dozens of ways that you can put your opt-in forms in front of people who visit your website. Some are unobtrusive and others are far more obvious, resembling a hard-sales technique. You need to decide which types of opt-in form placements you'll use to convert visitors into subscribers while ensuring your efforts don't annoy your visitors.

People come to your website to read or view your useful, meaningful, and relevant content. They don't come to be bombarded with opt-in forms that obscure the content they're looking for. Yes, obvious, in-your-face opt-in forms are likely to build your list more quickly, but they could annoy some people so much that they never visit your site again. You don't want to lose qualified leads, so weigh the benefits of generating a larger quantity of subscribers against the user experience visitors want and expect to have when they come to your website. Use a mix of placements to hit the sweet spot where you're not annoying visitors but still maximizing opt-ins.

Determining the best placements for your opt-in forms requires testing and tracking results. Chapter 12 discusses performance metrics in more detail, so be sure to read that for more information. Most important, understand that to optimize your opt-in form performance, you'll need to experiment not just with form design, copy, and offers but also with form placement and form type.

> **Tip**
> The opt-in form in your sidebar or any other location doesn't have to include a lead magnet or incentive offer. Whether or not you include one depends on your goals and is entirely up to you.

Opt-In Form Placements and Types

Opt-in forms can be displayed in various ways on your site. These are referred to as your form placements. Different placements use different types of forms, so you need to understand what types of forms are available to you either through your email marketing tool, your opt-in form tool, or your coding skills. Next, you need to make sure that the placement you want to use will fit and work properly on your website. With that in mind, here are some of the most commonly used form placements and types to consider using on your website if you're serious about building your email list.

Sidebar

A sidebar is the left or right column of content that appears on some web pages. Sidebar forms are extremely popular because they're unobtrusive and easy to create. Most email marketing tools allow you to create forms to place in your site's sidebar—simply copy some code and paste it into your website (e.g., in a text widget in the sidebar of a WordPress site) within minutes. You can see an example of a simple sidebar form created with OptinMonster in Figure 6–3.

FIGURE 6–3. Sidebar Opt-In Form

Many people expect to find a subscription form in your website's sidebar, so include one. You want it to be as easy as possible for people to subscribe to your email marketing list from any page of your website, and a form that appears on all (or many) pages that use a layout, which includes a sidebar, is an extremely effective way of accomplishing this goal.

Pop-Up

Pop-up opt-in forms are extremely effective; however, they can also be obtrusive. The key to making pop-up forms work for you is to use them strategically and sparingly. A pop-up form appears on a visitor's screen in front of the browser window. Pop-ups can be triggered to appear when someone first visits your website, when they visit a specific page, when they click on a specific link, when they scroll to a specific point on a page, or when they try to exit your site. You can see what a pop-up form created with GetResponse looks like in Figure 6–4.

Depending on the tool you're using to create your pop-up opt-in forms, your options for configuring when your pop-up appears will vary. The secret to success is ensuring your pop-up forms enhance the user experience on your website rather than hinder it. When you set up your pop-up opt-in forms, you should consider two things: behavior and frequency. Both are discussed in "Pop-Up Opt-In Form Triggers" on page 83.

Inline

Inline opt-in forms appear in the body of a web page. The position where you can display an inline form depends on your website and coding ability. For example, some

FIGURE 6–4. Pop-Up Opt-In Form

OPT-IN FORM TRIGGERS

Most email marketing providers and opt-in form tools allow you to set rules when certain types of opt-in forms are displayed to visitors, such as pop-ups, overlays/lightboxes, slide-ins, and full screen forms. Visitors' behaviors and frequency of visits to your website determine when these forms are triggered to display.

Behavior refers to the actions visitors take that trigger your opt-in forms to be shown. These behaviors could be visiting a specific page on your website (page-based trigger), being referred from a specific site to yours (referrer-based trigger), the type of device they're using to view your website (device-based trigger), if they try to leave your site (exit-intent trigger), and so on. You can see an example of an exit-intent, pop-up opt-in form in Figure 6–5.

FIGURE 6–5. Exit-Intent-Triggered, Pop-Up Opt-In Form

Again, check with your opt-in form tool to see what behaviors you can set as triggers to display your opt-in forms. Once configured, your opt-in form will be shown to anyone who visits your website and takes the action defined as your pop-up form trigger. For example, if you created a lead magnet ebook that is related to one of your products, it would make sense to display a pop-up form offering that ebook to anyone who tries to leave that product's page on your website. They might not be ready to buy now, but a relevant ebook that is useful and meaningful to them just might be

OPT-IN FORM TRIGGERS, continued

enough to push them further through the marketing funnel to the point that they will make a purchase.

Frequency refers to how often your triggered opt-in forms are displayed. This is particularly important to consider if people visit your website on a consistent basis. You don't want to show the same pop-up form to the same person every time they visit because it can become annoying. Instead, configure your triggered opt-in forms to display only to visitors who haven't seen them for a specific period. For example, you could configure your trigger rules so you don't show the same form to someone who visits your site for three days after they see it.

It's also a good idea to give visitors an opportunity to see your site before you interrupt their user experience with a triggered opt-in form. For example, you could time a welcome opt-in form to display 5, 10, or 30 seconds after a visitor lands on your site's home page. Waiting at least five seconds before displaying an obtrusive opt-in form makes it far less annoying because visitors have a chance to view your page and confirm that it's relevant to them before that page is covered with a form.

Both behavior and frequency must be tested to find the best settings for your opt-in forms to maximize submissions while minimizing their negative effects on the user experience. That means in addition to testing your offer, form copy, and form design, you also need to test when and how often your trigger-based forms are displayed to visitors.

WordPress themes might make it more challenging for you to display inline forms exactly where you want them to go than others. Simply copying and pasting text might not work perfectly, which means you'll need to be able to do some coding to ensure your forms look the way you want them to on your live site. You can see a sample inline form from OptinMonster in Figure 6–6 on page 85.

For example, you can display an inline opt-in form on your ecommerce checkout page, after every blog post, or after a specific blog post on your site. This is particularly effective when you're offering a lead magnet that is directly related to the topic of the blog post where it appears. The blog post could introduce visitors to a topic, and the lead magnet offered in the corresponding inline opt-in form might provide critical information about the next logical step people should take after reading the blog post.

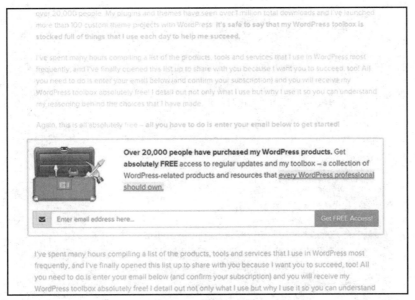

FIGURE 6–6. Inline Opt-In Form

Note: When an inline form is live on your website, the content surrounding it won't be grayed out like here, where the text has been faded so you can see the opt-in form.

This type of offer is often referred to as a content upgrade because you start by providing free information and then offer directly connected additional information in exchange for an email address.

Lightbox/Overlay

A lightbox or overlay is a type of opt-in form that eliminates distractions and can greatly increase the number of subscribers you get from your opt-in form. When your lightbox or overlay is shown on-screen, all other content is faded out in the background. Visitors are forced to interact with your opt-in form to continue using your website or even navigate to another website. An example created with OptinMonster is shown in Figure 6–7 on page 86.

Lightbox/overlay opt-in forms are usually triggered by a visitor action, such as clicking a link, scrolling, or exhibiting exit intent. You can learn more about triggers in "Opt-In Form Triggers" on page 83. Since lightbox/overlay forms require interaction, many marketers have great success adding a second button to the form. For example, rather than just including a button that says, "Yes, I want to subscribe" or another call to action, you can add a second button that says, "No, I don't want to get awesome tips in my inbox." In other words, rather than simply clicking the X to close the lightbox/ overlay, the visitor is more likely to read the copy and pick one of the two responses

FIGURE 6–7. Lightbox/Overlay Opt-In Form

provided. When the second button uses psychologically unappealing copy, opt-ins can increase significantly.

Full-Screen Welcome Mat, Exit Gate, Interstitial

A full-screen opt-in form covers the visitor's entire screen, which means they cannot view the content on your web page until they scroll past your form (usually by clicking a down arrow at the bottom of the form). Depending on when the full-screen opt-in form is displayed to visitors, it is either referred to as a welcome mat (displayed when visitors arrive at your site), exit gate (displayed when they try to leave your site), or interstitial (displayed when visitors navigate from one page to another within your site). You set the rules when the full-screen opt-in form is shown to visitors. You can see an example of a full screen opt-in form from Sumo in Figure 6–8 on page 87.

Full-screen opt-in forms can be extremely successful if you want to grow your email list quickly. However, they're also extremely intrusive and can negatively affect visitors' experiences on your website. Sometimes, visitors have trouble navigating past full-screen opt-in forms. They can also get annoyed when they're looking for content quickly and are stopped by a full-screen form, which can be cumbersome to close. As with all opt-in forms, you'll need to test the full-screen form on your website to determine if the uptick in subscribers outweighs the loss in traffic from annoyed visitors.

FIGURE 6–8. Full-Screen Opt-In Form

Floating Header or Footer Bar

A floating header opt-in form appears across the top of a web page when a visitor's mouse hovers near there. A floating footer bar does the same thing except it appears across the bottom of a web page when a visitor's mouse hovers near there. You can see an example of a floating footer bar from Sumo in Figure 6–9.

FIGURE 6–9. Floating Footer Bar Opt-In Form

A floating header or footer bar opt-in form is a great choice when you don't want your opt-in form to be too intrusive, but you want it to be easy for visitors to access. The floating header or footer bar opt-in form can also be displayed when visitors scroll on a page (depending on the tool you use to create it). Since it's sticky, it stays affixed to the bottom or top of the page no matter where visitors scroll. If pop-ups, lightboxes/overlays, and full-screen opt-in forms seem too pushy, then a floating header or footer bar might be a great option to maximize subscribers without overly annoying visitors.

Slide-In

Slide-in opt-in forms typically slide in from the right side of a visitor's screen when they scroll to a specific point on your web page. You determine the page and the rules for when the opt-in form will appear as discussed in "Opt-In Form Triggers" on page 83. You can get very strategic with your form and time it to display when the most relevant information is on the visitor's screen. As a result, they can be very effective in boosting highly targeted subscribers. You can see an example of a slide-in opt-in form from OptinMonster in Figure 6–10.

Slide-in opt-in forms are particularly effective when you're offering a content upgrade, discount, or an incentive or offer that is related to the content on the web page that a visitor is likely to be reading or viewing when the opt-in form appears. Therefore, create a complete campaign to go with slide-in opt-in forms to ensure you're offering the right thing to people who see it based on the corresponding page content and where they're likely to be in the marketing funnel.

FIGURE 6–10. Slide-In Opt-In Form

Mobile Pop-Ups

Mobile pop-up opt-in forms appear in front of your web page content on mobile devices. However, be very careful because Google and other search engines don't like anything that blocks web page content on mobile devices. This includes pop-up forms of any kind. You can see an example of a mobile pop-up form from OptinMonster in Figure 6–11.

FIGURE 6–11. Mobile Pop-Up Form

In fact, Google could penalize your site if you use obtrusive pop-up forms or other types of forms on your mobile site that could block the page content, such as floating headers and footer bars, slide-in forms, and full-screen forms. If your site is penalized, Google could send less traffic from searches to your site in the future. If you depend on Google to send visitors to your website (and most websites do), you might not want to risk it. Instead, use inline forms or in-text calls to action to increase opt-ins from your mobile audience.

Tip
Don't forget to collect opt-ins from your mobile app if you have one.

Landing Pages

A landing page is a web page created to motivate visitors to take a very specific action, which is referred to as a conversion. The conversion might be a sale, or it might be submitting an opt-in form to access a lead magnet, such as an ebook or webinar. While a landing page isn't a *type* of opt-in form, it is an essential part of building your email list, so it's important to understand what it is and how to use it.

You can create a landing page using a variety of tools, such as Leadpages, Unbounce, Instapage, or MailMunch. Some email marketing tools, like GetResponse, even include tools to create landing pages within their software so you don't need to invest in a separate tool to make them. Of course, you can also create custom landing pages if you know how to code them or pay a developer to create them for you. A landing page can be very simple like the template from Leadpages shown in Figure 6–12, or it can be a much

FIGURE 6–12. Short Landing Page

FIGURE 6–13. Long Landing Page

longer sales page filled with videos, testimonials, images, and more like the template from Instapage shown in Figure 6–13.

Typically, a long landing page is more effective for higher-value conversions. For example, you'll need more messages and details to persuade someone to click the button on your landing page to buy a product or schedule a free demo than you'll need to persuade them to click the button and download a free ebook. For

TEN LANDING PAGE FEATURES TO BOOST CONVERSIONS

1. A benefits-oriented headline

2. Descriptive subtitle and/or introduction copy

3. Eye-catching images and color

4. Bulleted lists rather than long paragraphs of copy

5. Testimonials from actual users or customers

6. A clear value proposition that answers the question, "What's in it for me?"

7. Messages that address a key pain point for visitors

8. An easy-to-find opt-in form (for long landing pages, the form should appear at the top and bottom of the page at a minimum)

9. Information about you to show you're a trustworthy source

10. A clear explanation of what they'll get and what happens after they submit your opt-in form

lesser-value incentives, such as a free checklist or ebook, use shorter landing pages that quickly and clearly communicate the benefits visitors receive when they provide their email address in the opt-in form. For more challenging conversions, follow the tips in "Ten Landing Page Features to Boost Conversions." You'll learn more about creating landing pages that convert in Chapter 7, but these tips give you an introduction to the critical elements your landing pages should include in addition to opt-in forms.

STEP 5: IMPROVE THE RESULTS OF YOUR ONLINE OPT-IN FORMS

Creating and displaying opt-in forms might not deliver instant results. Don't worry: that's extremely common. Remember, you need to drive visitors to your forms so they can evaluate your offers and decide whether those offers are of equal or lesser value to them than their email addresses. If your results are less than what you expect, consider increasing your marketing efforts to drive more traffic to your forms (if low traffic is the problem) or changing your offer (if conversion is the problem). In addition, you can try some of the tactics to improve the results of your online opt-in forms discussed in the remainder of this chapter. Most important, don't give up!

Display Multiple Opt-In Forms

An easy way to boost opt-ins is to display multiple opt-in forms on your website. For example, you can show the same offer on the same page or on different pages throughout your site. You can also display different offers on the same page or on different pages using page-level targeting techniques. This is an area where testing is critical. You don't want to inundate visitors with opt-in forms, so you'll need to experiment to find the perfect balance between a large number of opt-ins and too many forms.

One of the biggest mistakes you can make when building your email list is to assume people will find your opt-in form. Give them a variety of ways to find your forms, or you'll lose opportunities to grow your list. For example, consider using a welcome mat form, a sidebar form, an exit-intent pop-up form, and an inline form in your blog posts.

Use Calls to Action to Guide Visitors to Your Opt-In Forms

Sometimes, you won't be able to include a full opt-in form in certain areas of your website. Instead, you can use calls to action that guide visitors to your opt-in forms. For example, include a link with a call to action next to the submit button within the comment area of your blog posts. Add a call to action in your blog or website header as well as to your social media pages and profiles. You can even add a sign-up button to your Facebook Page.

Don't be afraid to ask your existing customers and email subscribers to share your opt-in form link with other people. After someone submits your opt-in form, create a strong call to action displayed on your thank-you page or confirmation email asking them to invite their friends to subscribe to your newsletter or download your lead magnet, too.

One of the most effective places to include an opt-in call to action message for ecommerce businesses is on the customer's shopping cart page. Here, they're already engaged with your brand, so it's the perfect time to invite them to subscribe to your list. But don't stop there. You should also include an opt-in call to action in your abandoned shopping cart campaigns. Even if someone isn't ready to make a purchase (and hopefully, you can change that person's mind with abandoned cart email campaigns), they might be ready to download your free lead magnet. A sale is better, but getting a prospect into your marketing funnel with an opt-in is better than nothing. Once they're on your list, you can continue to engage with them via email to try to convert them from a lead to a customer.

Offer Options

If your offer exceeds your audience's needs, you might have to offer different options to boost conversions. For example, if visitors are promised a daily email newsletter when they submit your opt-in form, that might equate to too much email for some people. If your email marketing provider and opt-in form tool allow it, offer multiple subscription offers, such as daily, weekly, or monthly.

Another example involves allowing visitors to choose not just the frequency of communications they'll receive from you but also the types of messages they'll receive. You can offer options to receive informational or promotional content, as well as options to receive messages related to specific topics. A health coach might offer options to receive content only about weight loss, exercise, recipes, or low-cholesterol diet tips. Assuming the health coach publishes enough content to fill all these topics, giving people this type of choice not only makes them happier but also allows the coach to segment the audience. If the coach knows that only some audience members are interested in weight loss, then promotional content related to weight-loss products can go directly to those people in the future.

Segment Your Audience and Offer Lead Magnet Choices

You can also segment your audience by offering lead magnet choices. For example, a pop-up opt-in form that appears when someone visits a specific page on your website could give people a choice to download one of two ebooks on topics relevant to the page topic but different from each other. A follow-up email marketing campaign could include a link to download the second ebook as well, but based on the visitor's choice when they submitted the form, you can segment that person using a specific interest. This is valuable information for future email marketing.

Test Your Opt-In Forms

The best way to test your opt-in forms to create the highest-converting forms possible is to conduct A/B split tests. In simplest terms, an A/B split test requires that you create two different versions of the same opt-in form. You change one element between the two forms, which is the element you're testing. For example, you could create two identical forms with different headlines. Everything is the same except one element. This is critical because if you change more than one element, you won't know which altered element was responsible for any differences you see in your results. If your email marketing provider or opt-in form tool offers split testing, you can create both forms (versions A and B) and publish both to display randomly in the same place. For example, you could display version A to 50 percent of visitors and version B to the other 50 percent. Once you have some data to compare the number of opt-ins received from each form, you can compare them and determine the winning form. Remove the underperforming form and show only the winning form to all future visitors.

You can perform A/B split tests anytime you want on a wide variety of elements. Some of the elements email marketers commonly test are:

- Headline
- Images (different images and forms with or without images)
- Colors
- Fonts
- Videos (different videos and forms with or without videos)
- Messages
- Size or color of the "submit" button
- Including or not including the email field directly on the form or just using a submit button and showing the fields on a separate page
- Shapes
- Placement on your website
- Timing when form is displayed
- Orientation (portrait vs. landscape)
- Position of elements such as the "submit" button

When running A/B split tests, make sure you run your tests long enough to confidently determine a winner. Also, just as scientists perform experiments multiple times before deeming results to be reliable, you should run your tests at least twice. Make sure you're testing both versions of your form at the same time rather than displaying one form for a few days and then the other form for a few days after that. Otherwise, you won't know if your results were affected by your opt-in form or by the audience visiting your site on different days.

Before You Begin Building Your Email List

Follow the five steps introduced in this chapter to build your email list: develop relevant offers, create effective opt-in forms, drive targeted visitors to your opt-in forms, show your offers to those visitors, and monitor performance to improve your results. Keep in mind there is a step you should take before you start thinking about your online opt-in forms. First, you need to make sure your website looks great to build trust and confidence.

It doesn't matter how great your opt-in forms look or how well they're displayed if visitors don't trust your website because no one will subscribe if your website doesn't meet their expectations. If your website looks untrustworthy and low quality, visitors are likely to assume everything else you offer is low quality, too. Instead, build a solid foundation with a great website and then strategically build your email list with well-designed and well-placed opt-in forms.

Chapter 7

Creating a Lead Magnet

L
ead magnets can be used to acquire, nurture, and convert prospects into buying customers. In simplest terms, a lead magnet is a bribe. It's a free incentive given in exchange for potential customers' email addresses. If the incentive is good enough, you could ask for even more information, such as name, address, phone number, and more. However, people put a high perceived value on their email addresses. They know that giving out their email addresses can lead to high volumes of unwanted email messages. Therefore, your lead magnets must be perceived by prospects as having an equal or greater value than their email addresses, or they won't be willing to exchange their email addresses for your lead magnets.

A great lead magnet attracts a qualified audience of relevant consumers. Most of the lead magnets used by marketers today are forms of digital content, such as an ebook, checklist, worksheet, tutorial, template, or other lead-generating value-add. Many of the email marketing programs you create will start with a lead magnet, but those programs will fail if you're not offering something your target audience wants enough to give you their contact information to get it. You can find a variety of resources, templates, and swipe files to create your own lead magnets and corresponding email marketing automations in

THE LEAD MAGNET EMAIL MARKETING PROCESS

Here's how a lead magnet email marketing program might work:

- You create a lead magnet that your target audience wants or needs.

- Your target audience provides their email addresses to you to download or access the lead magnet.

- You deliver the lead magnet to the people who opt into your list to get it.

- You follow up with ongoing email messages to nurture the relationship with your subscribers and convert them into buying customers.

Chapter 13 and the Appendix. For now, focus on what separates good lead magnets from bad ones.

GOOD LEAD MAGNETS VS. BAD LEAD MAGNETS

The good news is if you choose the right lead magnet and spread the word to the right people, your email list is practically guaranteed to grow. With that said, you need to understand what makes a lead magnet successful.

Successful Lead Magnets Succinctly Solve a Specific Problem

The best lead magnets provide useful, meaningful, or educational content quickly and clearly in a manner that is easy to digest so people can consume the content without feeling overwhelmed. Your lead magnets won't be successful if people don't use them. Instead, create lead magnets that do the thinking for your prospects. Don't communicate in general terms or about broad topics. Instead, choose a laser-focused topic and provide specific details to solve the prospect's primary problem related to that topic.

Successful Lead Magnets Are Relevant

Lead magnets must be relevant to your business, products, or services as well as to your target audience, or they won't attract qualified prospects. For example, if you own an accounting practice, then giving away an iPad as a lead magnet might not drive the best results for your business. You'll get a lot of opt-ins for it, but how many of those leads will be interested in your accounting services? A lead magnet should fill up your funnel, but if you're filling your funnel with people who will never buy from you, you're wasting your time marketing to them.

Instead, an accounting practice would have more success attracting qualified prospects with a tax preparation checklist or a hidden tax deductions cheat sheet. Someone who is interested in tax preparation and deductions is likely to have an interest in obtaining accounting services at some point. Once the accounting practice has qualified leads on its email list, it can use email nurturing and conversion funnels to push those leads further through the overall marketing funnel until they purchase.

Successful Lead Magnets Are Action-Oriented

Your lead magnets should be easy to follow and give prospects everything they need to complete a specific action or take the next step to reach a desired goal. As you already learned, a lead magnet that speaks in generalities won't be useful to your target audience. Instead, you need to do the work for your prospects.

If your lead magnet is a resource toolkit, provide links to all your recommended resources along with explanations of how and when to use them. If your lead magnet is a swipe file, make sure people know exactly how to use it immediately. If your lead magnet is a checklist, don't just provide ten things people should do. Instead, explain how to do each of those ten things. If your lead magnets aren't actionable, then they're not specific enough and are unlikely to be perceived as delivering adequate value.

Successful Lead Magnets Offer High Perceived Value

The perceived value of your lead magnets is the value that prospects attach to them. Since lead magnets are usually offered for free, prospects create a value for each lead magnet in their minds. This value is derived from the messages and images you use to promote each lead magnet. Remember, the perceived value must exceed your prospects' perceived value of their email addresses, or no one will want your lead magnet.

The best course of action is to always offer lead magnets that could be sold for a fee. If the content is good enough that someone would pay for it, then it should pass most prospects' perceived value tests. That means your lead magnets should be valuable. To that end, invest the time and money to create irresistible lead magnets that are better than what everyone else is offering to your target audience. You never want prospects to be disappointed after they receive your lead magnet because they'll project that negative experience onto other experiences with you. What does that mean? It means they probably won't buy from you because they'll expect to be disappointed based on their previous experience with your brand. A poor-quality, low-value lead magnet can do a lot of damage to your brand reputation and your business, so always plan on over-delivering.

Successful Lead Magnets Are Easy to Access

Deliverability matters, so make sure your lead magnets are easy for prospects to access once they opt in by providing their email addresses. Most email marketing providers make it easy for you to set up automations that automatically send a message to anyone who opts in to receive your lead magnet. That means as soon as they submit their email addresses using your opt-in form, they'll receive a message that includes your lead magnet or a link to download or access your lead magnet.

Accessibility also refers to the content *in* your lead magnet. This is where design matters. Perceived value plays a big role in the success of your lead magnet and subsequent email campaigns, so make sure your lead magnet looks like a high-quality product. It's not the "Mona Lisa," but it is representative of your brand and sets expectations for your brand in consumers' minds. For example, make sure your ebooks, guides, reports, white papers, and other written lead magnets are formatted for easy readability with a lot of white space, quality images, bulleted lists, and headings. User experience should be a top priority as you create lead magnets.

Successful Lead Magnets Are Not Entirely Self-Promotional

Lead magnets should be useful, meaningful, educational, entertaining, or indirectly sales-related. They should not be directly self-promotional. How many people do you know who would trade their email addresses in exchange for an ad? As a consumer, would you make that exchange? Most people would not. In fact, most people would be angry if they were promised something useful, meaningful, educational, entertaining, or helpful and ended up getting an ad—whether or not they gave up their email addresses for it.

The purpose of a lead magnet is to build your email marketing list so you can start developing a relationship with prospects that can eventually turn into sales and brand loyalty. If you start by baiting them with something useful, then switch the deliverable with something promotional, they're unlikely to stay on your email list for long. In fact, they might even tell their friends, family, and social media connections about their bad experience. That kind of negative word-of-mouth can destroy your brand.

Rather than directly promoting your business, brand, products, or services in your lead magnets, demonstrate your thought leadership. Think of your lead magnets as the first step to building a relationship with potential customers so they can develop trust in your brand. This doesn't mean your lead magnets shouldn't include any promotional content, but the promotional content should be secondary to the "meat" of the lead magnet. For example, include a page at the end of an ebook that promotes your business as the solution to the prospect's problem that motivated them to download the ebook in the first place, or include a message in the footer of a checklist lead magnet with a URL to learn more about the solution your business offers. If your content is great, prospects won't mind a subtle promotion within your lead magnet.

STEPS TO CREATING A LEAD MAGNET

Creating a successful lead magnet doesn't need to take a lot of time. In fact, simple checklists and cheat sheets that take less than 30 minutes to create are often some of the most successful lead magnets for acquiring new leads at the top of the marketing funnel and nurturing leads in the middle of the marketing funnel. They're easily consumable and immediately actionable. What's not to love? Ebooks, white papers, guides, and other lead magnets that take longer to create can be just as successful, but you need to consider your goals, your target audience, and their immediate needs to determine which type of lead magnet will deliver the best results.

Think of it this way: A lead at the top of the funnel who has never heard of your brand, products, or services is far more likely to give you their email address to enter a contest, access a free template, or download a swipe file that will save them time and effort than they are to sign up for a webinar or download a case study. You need to start to build a relationship and trust in your brand before you can expect someone to schedule an hour of their time with you for a webinar or be interested enough in your products and services to read a case study. These types of lead magnets are usually more effective for nurturing leads in the middle of the funnel and converting leads at the bottom of the funnel. This isn't always the case. A checklist could be a great lead magnet for prospects at the bottom of the funnel, or a webinar could be successful when used to acquire leads at the top of the funnel. You can see an example of a worksheet used as a lead magnet in Figure 7–1 on page 102.

Most important, lead magnets can attract new prospect to all parts of the marketing funnel depending on where a prospect is in the buyer journey. They can also be used to attract existing leads on your email list to different parts of the marketing funnel. For example, they could be used to pull a prospect from the top of the funnel to the middle or from the middle of the funnel to the bottom. The lead magnet you use depends entirely on your goals and audience.

Choose Your Lead Magnet

The first step is to pick a lead magnet to offer to prospective customers. That means you need to know who your target audience is and what they need so you create a lead magnet that they'll actually want. Start by asking yourself these three questions:

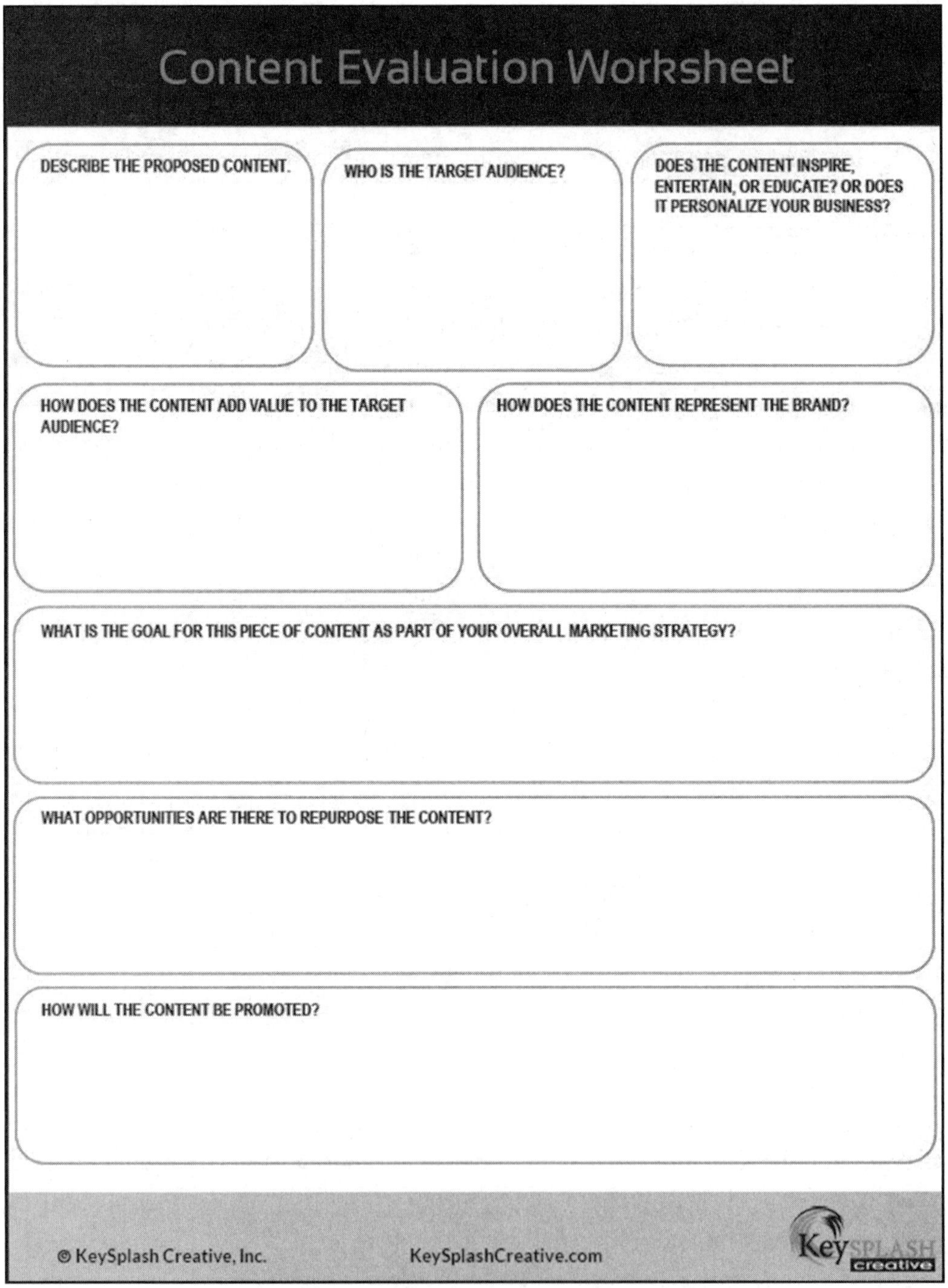

Content Evaluation Worksheet

| DESCRIBE THE PROPOSED CONTENT. | WHO IS THE TARGET AUDIENCE? | DOES THE CONTENT INSPIRE, ENTERTAIN, OR EDUCATE? OR DOES IT PERSONALIZE YOUR BUSINESS? |

HOW DOES THE CONTENT ADD VALUE TO THE TARGET AUDIENCE?

HOW DOES THE CONTENT REPRESENT THE BRAND?

WHAT IS THE GOAL FOR THIS PIECE OF CONTENT AS PART OF YOUR OVERALL MARKETING STRATEGY?

WHAT OPPORTUNITIES ARE THERE TO REPURPOSE THE CONTENT?

HOW WILL THE CONTENT BE PROMOTED?

© KeySplash Creative, Inc.   KeySplashCreative.com   KeySPLASH creative

FIGURE 7–1. Example Lead Magnet: Worksheet

1. What problem or pain point does my target audience have?
2. What can I teach my target audience that will make things easier or better for them, or what can I give them that will make them happier?
3. Are my products or services relevant to this problem or pain point, and can my target audience solve this problem or pain point with my products or services?

Once you answer these three questions, think of ways to solve your target audience's problem through content that you provide in a lead magnet. For example, if a massage therapist's target audience has a problem with back pain from sitting at their computers all day, they could offer a video lead magnet with exercises to alleviate that specific pain or a shopping list filled with natural herbs and essential oils that can be used to ease back pain.

Once you think you've selected your lead magnet, ask yourself these five questions:

1. Does my target audience want this?
2. Does my lead magnet provide a tangible benefit or result for my target audience?
3. Will my target audience be satisfied when they receive this lead magnet? Is its value worth the perceived value people put on their email addresses?
4. Does this lead magnet present my brand and business as trustworthy, helpful, and knowledgeable rather than self-promotional?
5. Does this lead magnet solve my target audience's problem or pain point, giving actionable information that makes their lives easier, better, or happier?

Your answers to these questions will tell you whether you've chosen the right lead magnet or if you need to start over. Now, let's back up and consider the five primary types of lead magnets you can choose from: useful (helpful), meaningful (emotional), educational (practical), entertaining (enjoyable), and sales (profitable). Depending on your target audience and where prospects are in your overall marketing funnel, the lead magnet you choose to create will vary.

Useful Lead Magnets

Useful lead magnets are helpful. They help prospects solve a problem or ease a pain point. These lead magnets are created to help people save time, money, or effort because they address a problem or pain point and offer an actionable solution. That's why useful lead magnets are often referred to as silver bullets. When someone needs help, a useful lead magnet gives them exactly what they need in a concise and easy-to-use format. In other words, the lead magnet does all the hard work for them. For example, an advertising agency might offer a tutorial to create a specific type of Facebook ad that is proven to drive results. Other examples include checklists, cheat sheets, templates, swipe files, and tutorials.

Meaningful Lead Magnets

Meaningful lead magnets elicit emotions. The vast majority of purchase decisions are based at least in part on emotions. Furthermore, establishing an emotional connection between prospects and your brand is one of the most powerful ways to move them through the marketing funnel. Relationships built on trust are a brand's ultimate goal. Therefore, creating lead magnets that tap into prospect's emotions can establish a strong connection between your audience and your brand. They have a meaning for consumers that transcends tangible results. For example, a life coach could offer a collection of journal prompts as a lead magnet. Other examples of meaningful lead magnets include videos, images, audio content, quotes, quizzes, and success stories.

Educational Lead Magnets

Educational lead magnets are highly practical. They provide practical steps and instructions to teach prospects how to accomplish specific tasks or develop strategies. Educational lead magnets are particularly useful in industries with long sales cycles, complex industries, and highly regulated industries. For example, most business owners don't know how important it is to trademark their brand names. An intellectual property attorney could create a lead magnet that teaches entrepreneurs why they should trademark their brand names and how to do it. This type of lead magnet establishes the attorney as an expert in their field and helps to build trust between the attorney's brand and prospects. Of course, educational lead magnets also indirectly promote your products or services because once prospects learn about a topic, your products or services are positioned perfectly to help them take the next steps to solve their problems or address their pain points. Other examples of educational lead magnets include ebooks, guides, courses, tutorials, reports, videos, and webinars.

Entertaining Lead Magnets

Entertaining lead magnets do exactly what the name implies. They entertain people. Entertaining lead magnets are enjoyable and are used to nurture prospects by strengthening their relationships with your brand. While not appropriate for every industry, they are very effective in a variety of industries, such as travel, fashion, and personal coaching. For example, a hair salon could send prospects a quiz to determine the best haircut for them. Other examples of entertaining lead magnets include quizzes, videos, images, cartoons, and contests.

Sales Lead Magnets

Sales lead magnets are created with a single purpose—to convert leads at the bottom of the marketing funnel into buying customers. To that end, they're focused directly on a lead's specific problem or pain point and make it obvious that the solution is your products or services without being overly self-promotional. While it's less common to use lead magnets to acquire leads at the bottom of the funnel, the buyer journey isn't always linear. That means prospects who are close to making a buying decision could find your brand and business when they've already reached the last steps of the buyer journey.

40 LEAD MAGNETS YOU CAN CREATE

1. Checklist
2. Worksheet
3. Workbook
4. Cheat sheet
5. Ebook
6. Webinar
7. Timeline
8. Mini video course
9. Template
10. Calendar
11. Recipe
12. Swipe file
13. White paper
14. Video
15. Resource list
16. Plan or planner
17. Tutorial
18. Sample files or documents
19. Report
20. Infographic
21. Case study
22. Spreadsheet
23. How-to guide
24. Toolkit
25. Contest/giveaway
26. Discount or coupon code
27. Free trial
28. Free demonstration
29. Free coaching or consulting session
30. Audio content
31. Images
32. Quotes or quote collections
33. Email course
34. Free sample box
35. Script
36. PDF version of a popular blog post
37. Transcript of an interview or podcast
38. Presentation
39. Scorecard
40. Resource library subscription

Rather than missing the opportunity to connect with them, a sales lead magnet can delay their final purchase decision by adding your products or services to the evaluation process. Ultimately, they might choose your brand over the others they've been considering, but you'd lose that sale if you hadn't tried to connect with them in the final stages of their purchase process. For example, a photographer could offer a deep discount on wedding packages as a lead magnet to highly targeted audiences at the bottom of the funnel. Other examples of effective sales lead magnets include white papers, ebooks, reports, free trials, free demonstrations, guides, case studies, coupon codes, and free coaching or consulting sessions.

Create Your Lead Magnet

Once you know what your lead magnet will be, it's time to create it. Don't sacrifice quality for price or time. The quality of your lead magnet plays a critical part in the perception of your brand that is created in people's minds when they access it. This perception will directly affect their desire to engage with your brand or buy from your business in the future. First impressions matter a lot, so hire an experienced copywriter and a great designer to create your lead magnet for you if you can afford it. If your budget is too tight to get professional help, there are tools available that will enable you to create your own lead magnets. Following are some recommendations to get you started.

Design Tools

Each of the tools listed below are free, offer free trials, or are available at affordable costs.

- *Canva* (www.canva.com) is easy to use and includes many free images and icons that you can include in your checklist, worksheet, cheat sheet, ebook, and other lead magnet designs.
- *Stencil* (https://getstencil.com) is also easy to use and offers a large number of icons you can use.
- *PicMonkey* (www.picmonkey.com) is not only easy to use, but it also offers a variety of unique effects that you can apply to your text and images to make them stand out.
- *Paint.net* (www.getpaint.net) is an excellent free tool for Windows users as an alternate to the pricey Photoshop software from Adobe.
- *Gimp* (www.gimp.org) is another free alternative to Photoshop, which both Windows and Mac users can use.
- *Inkscape* (https://inkscape.org/en) is a free alternative to Adobe Illustrator for Windows, Mac, and Linux users.

When you choose images, fonts, and icons to use in your lead magnet designs, be sure to read the licensing information. The license explains exactly what you can use an image, font, or icon for and if you need to provide attribution to the owner in your design. You don't want to violate any copyright laws, so err on the side of caution when it comes to using other people's work in your designs.

> **Definition**
> *Royalty-free images* are images that you pay a one-time fee to use in a specific design per a license agreement with the owner. No ongoing payments (royalties) are required.

Image, Icon, and Font Sources

Following are a variety of websites where you can find free and affordable images, icons, and fonts for your lead magnet designs.

- *Bigstock* (www.bigstockphoto.com) offers a large selection of royalty-free images you can use in your lead magnets without worrying about infringing on other people's copyrights.
- *PhotoSpin* (www.photospin.com) offers fewer images than Bigstock but with a lower subscription price tag.
- *Creative Market* (https://creativemarket.com) is a website where creative people offer their own images, fonts, icons, and more for sale.
- *Iconmonster* (https://iconmonstr.com) is a great site to find simple icons for your lead magnet designs.
- *MyFonts* (www.myfonts.com) offers a large selection of fonts you can use in your lead magnet designs.

Infographic and Visualization Tools

Infographics and data visualizations look complex, but you can create them with the right tools. Here are some to try:

- *Visme* (www.visme.co) makes it easy to create amazing looking infographics, presentations, charts, graphics, and reports using a variety of templates.
- *Piktochart* (https://piktochart.com) offers templates to create infographics, reports, and printables.
- *Venngage* (https://venngage.com) offers templates to create infographics, reports, posters, promotional materials, and social media visuals.
- *Creately* (https://creately.com) makes it easy for you to create great-looking diagrams, Gantt charts, flowcharts, and more.
- *MindMeister* (www.mindmeister.com) is a tool to create visually appealing mind maps.

Video and Audio Tools

Creating video and audio content requires a few different types of tools, including recording and editing software, such as Camtasia (www.techsmith.com/video-editor.html) or Screencast-O-Matic (https://screencast-o-matic.com), a video camera, and a microphone. You also need somewhere to host your video and audio content where people can play it back. Since these files are usually very large, it's best not to host them on your own website hosting account. Instead, use a third-party video host, such as YouTube (www.youtube.com), Vimeo (https://vimeo.com), or Dailymotion (www.dailymotion.com/us). If your budget allows it, you can host your videos using Wistia (https://wistia.com), which includes built-in lead-generation tools that integrate with most popular email marketing providers' tools.

Design Your Landing Page and Opt-in Forms

With your lead magnet ready, it's time to give it a home online—a place where you can send prospects to learn about it and provide their email addresses to access it. Depending on your goals for your lead magnet and how you plan to promote it, you might be able to create one or more opt-in forms as discussed in Chapter 6, which you can display in multiple places on your website. For example, if you're offering a content upgrade to people who read a specific blog post on your website, then an inline, pop-up, or lightbox opt-in form would be perfect choices. When someone visits that blog post, they'll see your opt-in form, learn about your lead magnet, and have the option to easily request it.

Sometimes, your lead magnet will need its own web page, so you have a URL to send people to learn about it and request it. For example, if you're advertising a free ebook using Facebook ads, you need to include a URL with the ad that people can click on to learn more and opt in to receive it. In that case, you should create a landing page for your lead magnet. As you learned in Chapter 6, a landing page is a special type of web page that is dedicated to promoting one specific thing, such as a lead magnet. Lead magnet landing pages are filled with promotional messages and useful information about the lead magnet so visitors are motivated to submit their email addresses

> **Tip**
> If your text and image lead magnet files are large, you might not want to host them on your own website. Instead, you could upload them to Dropbox (www.dropbox.com) or Google Drive (https://drive.google.com) and share them (following the instructions provided by Dropbox or Google Drive) so anyone with the link can see them. Alternately, some email service providers allow you to host your lead magnet files on their servers as part of your email marketing campaigns and automations.

to download the lead magnet. They're visually appealing and devoid of extraneous links and information that detract from the page's single purpose of promoting the lead magnet.

If you're able to design and code web pages or have the budget to hire a professional to develop landing pages for you, then you're all set. Otherwise, you can use an affordable landing page tool to create professional-looking landing pages. Check out "Landing Page Templates for Inspiration" on page 110 to view lead magnet landing page templates from some of the most popular landing page tool providers.

Your landing pages should include an opt-in form for lead generation. If you're using landing pages for sales conversion goals, then you might want to include a button or link with a strong call to action on your landing page that leads visitors to another page (such as an online shopping cart) where they can complete that action (such as making a purchase). You learned about creating opt-in forms in Chapter 6, and most landing page tools make it easy to integrate their opt-in forms with your email marketing tool. To develop your actual landing pages, you need to understand how to create designs and content that make people want your lead magnet enough to submit your opt-in form to get it. To ensure the landing pages you create deliver the best results, you need to follow ten rules of landing page design.

1. Stay Laser-Focused on a Single, Specific Goal

Your landing page should have one specific goal. This goal is some type of action that you want visitors to take. For lead generation, this desired action is submitting the opt-in form on the page. Before you create your landing page, ask yourself what you want visitors who land on your page to do. That action should be the only thing you talk about on your page and the only thing visitors can *do* on your page.

2. Prioritize Your Messages with the Most Important Information above the Fold

Don't make people scroll to learn what you're offering and why it should matter to them. Your most important messages should

---

Definition

A *content upgrade* is a type of lead magnet that is tied to a specific page or blog post on your website. When someone visits the trigger page, an opt-in form, which could be inline, pop-up, or another type, invites visitors to submit their email addresses in exchange for a highly relevant incentive. For example, the lead magnet could be an ebook explaining the next steps the visitor should take after reading a blog post, or it could be a free trial or coupon depending on where visitors are likely to be in the overall marketing funnel when they visit the page.

LANDING PAGE TEMPLATES FOR INSPIRATION

The most popular tools to create landing pages offer templates that have been proven to convert well. Some of these tools include Leadpages, Instapage, and Unbounce. If you use WordPress, OptimizePress is another popular choice. You can view the landing page templates offered by each of these tools by visiting the URLs listed below:

- *Leadpages*: www.leadpages.net/templates
- *Instapage*: https://instapage.com/landing-page-templates
- *Unbounce*: https://unbounce.com/landing-page-templates
- *OptimizePress*: https://marketplace.optimizepress.com

be above the fold so there is no chance that visitors can miss them. Throughout the rest of your landing page, work down through your message priority list. In other words, lead with your most powerful messages and use the remainder of your landing page to provide important supporting information. Be sure to repeat your powerful, action-oriented messages to keep visitors engaged as they read.

3. Write an Irresistible Headline

Use your landing page headline to answer the most important question in copywriting. This is the question that every prospect will ask when they arrive on your landing page: "What's in it for me?" Be clear and succinct. Visitors should instantly understand that the information on the landing page addresses their problem or pain point and the solution they've been looking for is at their fingertips if they follow your call to action (such as submitting your opt-in form).

4. Provide Specific Benefits to Your Target Audience

Remember, consumers don't care about brands or companies. They care about what brands and companies can do for them. They care about how brands and companies can help them, make their lives better, or make their lives easier. Therefore, it's safe to

> **Tip**
> If you're driving people to your landing page through ads and other promotional tactics, make sure the ad copy you use is directly related to the landing page headline so visitors immediately understand that they're in the right place.

assume that few people care about your lead magnet. They care about the benefits they'll get when they download and use it.

With that in mind, your landing page should clearly highlight the benefits prospects will get when they access your lead magnet. Will they save time or money? Will they reduce their stress level or improve their peace of mind? Will they be able to acquire more customers of their own or make more money? Don't assume they know how your lead magnet benefits them when they read about its features. Instead, you need to make sure they understand the benefits with no room for confusion.

5. Explain Desirable Features

What are the most desirable features of your lead magnet? In copywriting, benefit messages are always more powerful than feature messages, but that doesn't mean your audience isn't interested in the features they'll get from your lead magnet. With that said, provide a bulleted list of features, such as a list of chapters for an ebook or the topics covered in a webinar. Think of it this way: benefits sell, but features prove that the lead magnet can deliver those benefits.

6. Provide a Clear Call to Action and Repeat It

What do you want people to do when they visit your landing page? For lead generation, you most likely want them to submit your opt-in form and provide their email addresses. This call to action should be clear and obvious. That means it should appear above the fold and again at the bottom of your landing page (if it requires scrolling to view the entire page) at a minimum. If your landing page is long and requires a lot of scrolling, it should also appear in the middle of the page. The call to action should always be easily accessible no matter where a visitor is on your page.

7. Include Relevant Images and Videos

Images and videos add color and interest to your landing page, but they can also communicate important messages visually. Charts, icons, screenshots, ebook covers, presentation slides, images of your checklists, and so on can provide additional information, and they can pique visitors' interest in your lead magnet. A checklist sounds great, but when a visitor can see a small image of the checklist, they'll better understand the quality of the lead magnet. This can increase their trust and your conversion rate.

With that said, don't go overboard with images and videos. Just as all the text messages on your landing page should be relevant to the page's specific goal, so should images and videos. Every element on the page should support the call to action and make visitors believe that following it will help them, address their pain point, or solve their problem. If an element on your page doesn't move visitors closer to taking that action, delete it.

8. Use Proper Formatting for a Focused User Experience

Since landing pages are focused on a single, specific goal, there should be no distractions from your call to action. Remove your website's top navigation bar and any other irrelevant links, images, text, and so on. Your design should use a single-column and a lot of white space to ensure your key messages are easy to see. Use bulleted lists, headings, and subheadings to guide visitors through your copy. Always include a hero image at the top of your landing pages. This large image could be the cover of your ebook, report, or white paper. It could be an image of your checklist, cheat sheet, or worksheet. It could be a screenshot from your video or presentation. The image should be of your lead magnet if possible so visitors can see what they'll get in exchange for their email addresses.

9. Offer Social Proof

One of the best ways to build trust with visitors is to include testimonials on your landing page. This type of social proof makes visitors feel confident that your lead magnet is valuable enough to provide their email addresses to you. If other people had success with your lead magnet, then visitors are more likely to think they'll have success with it, too. As a result, they're more likely to follow your call to action and submit your opt-in form. Ideally, your testimonials should include people's full names and photos, as well as their company names so visitors know the testimonials are real. Always ask people for permission before you use their testimonials, names, and photos on any page of your website, including your landing pages.

10. Display an Easy-to-Complete Opt-In Form

It should be extremely easy for people to follow your call to action and opt into your email list from your landing page. To increase conversions, keep the form simple with as few fields as possible. Simply asking for an email address will yield the best results, but if you need more information, you can include fields to get that information in your opt-in form. Just remember, while it can be tempting to ask for a lot of information in your opt-in form, your opt-in rate will decrease with each additional field you add. Your lead magnet must be perceived as having a very high value for people to be willing to provide a lot of their personal information in exchange for it.

Set up an Email Automation to Deliver Your Lead Magnet

With your lead magnet created and your landing page published, it's time to create an automated delivery sequence to go with it. Specifically, you need to create a sequence of messages to deliver the lead magnet to people who request it and then follow up with those people after the lead magnet has been delivered. You can learn more about developing lead magnet automations (also referred to as email conversion funnels) in Chapter 8 and find swipe files to write your own messages in Chapter 13. For now, think about how you can use email marketing to deliver your lead magnet and begin to develop a relationship and brand trust with each new subscriber to your email list.

Your lead magnet email sequence should be scheduled to send the first message with a link to download the lead magnet as soon as someone submits the opt-in form. This message should thank the person for requesting the lead magnet, and it can provide any details they need to download and use it immediately. Two to three days later, a second message should be sent automatically as part of this email sequence. This message can vary depending on the action taken by the subscriber when they received the first message. If they clicked the link and downloaded the lead magnet, they should get a message asking if they have questions or need additional help. If they didn't click the link, this message should remind them what they're missing out on by not using the lead magnet.

A few days later, a third message can go out with another useful piece of information related to the content in the lead magnet. You can also include links to relevant resources on your website, such as blog posts or other content. The key is to continue offering them useful, meaningful information to nurture the relationship. About a week later, you could send a final message reminding them that you're available if they have questions or need help. For people who haven't downloaded the ebook, you could remind them of the benefits one more time. After this email sequence ends, make sure these new subscribers are included in your email newsletter and other email campaigns in the future.

Promote Your Lead Magnet

If no one knows your lead magnet exists, no one will opt in to receive it. You need to promote your lead magnet on your blog (write a blog post about it and include a link to it at the end of all your new blog posts), your social media posts, and any content you write for other websites. Investing in digital advertising can significantly affect your lead magnet conversions. Facebook ads are particularly effective since targeting is so useful, but Google AdWords and other ad networks can also be successful. Don't just promote your lead magnet once and never mention it again. Only a small percentage of your target audience will see your messages, posts, and ads the first time you promote it. Instead, you need to talk about it and invest in online advertising multiple times to truly drive traffic to it and motivate a large number of people to request it.

You can also promote your lead magnet through your social media profiles by creating special cover photos for your profiles and pages on Twitter, Facebook, LinkedIn, and so on that hype the lead magnet and show the URL to your landing page. Another idea is to hype the lead magnet at the beginning of your Twitter, Facebook, and LinkedIn bios and About sections along with the URL to your landing page. If you participate in online forums or Facebook or LinkedIn Groups where your target audience spends time, include a link to your lead magnet in your relevant comments or your own signature block. If you answer questions on Quora.com and your lead magnet is relevant to one of your answers, include a link to it within your answer or at least in your bio. You can also reach out to your social media communities and online influencers you know who have the eyes and ears of your target audience and ask them to share the link to your landing page with their online connections. Don't be afraid to get creative with your promotional efforts.

Track Your Results

If you've integrated your landing page, opt-in forms, Google Analytics (or the website analytics tool of your choice), your online advertising, and your email marketing tool, then tracking the results of your lead magnet and associated marketing campaigns to promote your lead magnet isn't difficult. You want to focus on which marketing investments are driving the most traffic to your landing page and which are resulting in the most opt-ins for your lead magnet. You also want to track the ratio of your landing page visitors to opt-ins and the ratio of opt-ins to the number of people who clicked the link in your delivery email message and downloaded the lead magnet. Look for conversion rates at each step and the cost to acquire each of your leads.

Conducting A/B split testing (discussed in more detail in Chapter 6) of your opt-in forms, landing pages, ads, and so on will help you improve results along the way rather than waiting until you've invested a lot of money in advertising to discover that the lead magnet isn't working, the landing page needs to be revised, or your ads are ineffective. Analytics and testing email marketing campaigns is covered in depth in Chapter 12, so be sure to read it closely to get a better understanding of performance tracking.

MOVING FROM LEAD MAGNETS TO EMAIL MARKETING FUNNELS

With your lead magnet, landing page, and opt-in forms ready to go, it's time to focus on creating email marketing funnels to acquire, nurture, and convert leads to customers. You do this by creating specific email marketing funnels or automated sequences (also called automations) that generate leads to build your email marketing list, build relationships with leads already on your email marketing list, and convince leads on your list to buy from you. Move on to Chapter 8 for all the details about developing an email marketing conversion funnel.

Developing an Email Marketing Conversion Funnel

There are three purposes for email marketing programs: to acquire, nurture, and convert leads into customers by making a sale. These, along with various types of email marketing funnels, are discussed in detail in Chapter 5. Now, let's get more specific and talk about the big ta-da—converting emails to actions like sales. To create programs for acquiring, nurturing, and converting leads, email marketers often set up individual email marketing conversion funnels. The terminology can get a bit confusing, so think of it this way. Any type of email funnel you create helps move prospects through your overall marketing funnel from the top where prospects aren't close to being ready to buy from you all the way to the bottom where they just need a little nudge to make a purchase. Similarly, many of the email funnels you create will be built for a specific conversion. That conversion doesn't have to be a purchase. In other words, email funnels created to acquire or nurture prospects are built to motivate those prospects to take some kind of action. When they take that action, the conversion has been completed. These email funnels are referred to as *email conversion funnels*.

Therefore, email conversion funnels can be thought of as any automated sequence of messages (i.e., automations) created to motivate prospects to complete an action that moves them further through the overall marketing funnel. In other words, you have lots of little email

EMAIL CONVERSION FUNNEL IDEAS

Ideas for Acquisition Email Conversion Funnels

- Low-risk lead magnet opt-in funnel (checklist, cheat sheet, template, etc.)
- Contest or giveaway funnel
- Content upgrade funnel

Ideas for Nurturing Email Conversion Funnels

- Deep-dive lead magnet opt-in funnel (ebook, mini course, guide, etc.)
- Webinar funnel
- New product launch funnel

Ideas for Conversions (Sales) Email Conversion Funnels

- Free trial or demonstration funnel
- Free call for coaching or consulting funnel
- Post-purchase upsell funnel

conversion funnels inside your overall marketing funnel, and each one is used to push people to the bottom of that overall marketing funnel. They're also used to keep people from falling out of the overall marketing funnel.

KEY CONSIDERATIONS WHEN DEVELOPING EMAIL CONVERSION FUNNELS

Now it's time to bring a few of the concepts from earlier chapters together. During the development process, if you want your email marketing conversion funnels to be as successful as possible, consider these five key email marketing best practices. Whether you're marketing to consumers or other businesses, and regardless of the industry you're in, these five considerations have a direct effect on the success rates of your email marketing efforts.

1. Timing

Email marketing funnels include a sequence of messages that are automatically sent out (or "dripped") at specific times as we discussed in Chapter 5. You set this timing up when you create the automation in your email marketing tool. Since the power of email conversion funnels is in their ability to remind, engage, and persuade contacts to take specific actions, the timing of when people receive your messages matters a lot. If you were speaking with someone, would you tell them something and then continue to remind them every five minutes? If you needed to call a prospect to close a sale, would you call them twice a day, every day, or every other day? How often is too often?

Most email recipients act on a message within 24 hours. Therefore, an automated sequence of messages should be configured to send messages every two days unless there is a deadline or other urgent reason that requires messages in your funnel to be sent more frequently. You can extend the number of days between messages when you reach the third message in a sequence so it doesn't seem like you're spamming people with too many messages. For example, the timing of a two-week email funnel might look like Figure 8–1.

The timing has no strict rules. Your goal is to find the right balance that your audience will accept between staying in front of your contacts and looking like a spammer. Keep in mind, email marketing funnels that are built to move recipients to take a specific action aren't like other types of email marketing campaigns. First, they last for a limited time. Second, they usually offer something of value for recipients.

> **Tip**
> When figuring the frequency of your email funnel messages, consider the time of day they're sent to recipients. If your email marketing provider allows it, schedule messages to go out early in the morning, shortly after lunch, or in the early evening when open rates are traditionally highest. Furthermore, schedule messages to be sent based on each contact's time zone.

Message Number	Day Sent
Message 1	Day 1
Message 2	Day 3
Message 3	Day 5
Message 4	Day 10
Message 5	Day 14

FIGURE 8–1. Two-Week Funnel Timing

This is very different than an informational newsletter filled with links to your most recent blog posts. If recipients received your newsletter every day or every other day, that would likely be too much, and many would unsubscribe or request less frequent delivery. They're far more tolerant of receiving the content in email funnels if the offer is highly relevant to them.

2. Offer

The heart of every email conversion funnel is the offer to your target audience—what they'll get in exchange for taking the action you want. As you've learned in previous chapters, your offer must be extremely relevant to the target audience and highly desirable, or they won't be motivated to act. In other words, your email conversion funnel won't convert. Therefore, spend time researching what your audience wants and needs. Search Google, online forums, question sites like Quora.com, and your competitors' content to find the problems and pain points that your target audience is seeking solutions for, and then offer those solutions in your email conversion funnels.

For example, you could create an email conversion funnel to motivate people to read your new case study, join your upcoming webinar, watch your latest video, or buy your product or service. The trick is matching the offer to the audience depending on where they are in the buyer journey and where you want to move them to in your overall marketing funnel. Email conversion funnels are very flexible, and you can customize them to match your goals. But you must remember that your target audience's wants and needs are always the top priority, or your conversion rates will suffer. Audience segmentation can help significantly in terms of improving your conversion rates. You can learn more about list segmentation in Chapter 9.

3. Subject Line

It could be argued that the subject line of each message in your email conversion funnels is the most important element. The reason is simple. If your subject line isn't powerful enough to convince people to click and open your messages, you have no way of converting those people. Your subject lines should be short enough to fully display in most email inboxes without being truncated. With that in mind, keep your subject lines shorter than 50 characters. The best subject lines are interesting and pique the recipient's curiosity. Address the audience's pain point and the solution you're offering, but keep your subject line clear.

It's also very important that the content of your messages matches the expectations created by your subject lines. Not only will recipients be unhappy when they click through a subject line to discover the content of the message is unrelated, but doing so can also destroy your chance of creating brand trust. Ultimately, you could lose conversions because of it and increase unsubscribes. Testing different subject lines through A/B split testing and creating different subject lines for unique segments of your audience can also help increase the open rate. The more people who open, the more potential conversions.

4. Design and Messages

Make sure your messages are well designed and look professional to create the perception of quality and build trust with recipients. Furthermore, they should be optimized for all devices. This is particularly important since more than half of email messages are opened on mobile devices today.

When it comes to writing your messages, unless your product or service is complex, shorter messages are almost always better in email marketing. That doesn't mean long messages don't work. Many email marketers have great success with long-form messages, but if those messages aren't written well, they won't help to boost your conversions. The truth is, most people don't want to spend a lot of time reading email messages, so keeping your messages succinct is a good rule of thumb. Just make sure your messages are compelling, action-oriented, and tap into recipients' emotions. Explain what recipients get when they follow your call to action and how that action benefits them by addressing their pain point or solving their problem. In addition, be sure to use a real reply-to email address and your real name in your messages and signature to improve the authenticity and trust factor.

Segmenting your list and writing copy specific to each niche audience can significantly increase your conversions as can using personalization and dynamic content. According to Epsilon's "Q1 2016 Email Trends and Benchmarks" report, personalized email messages can increase click rates by 241 percent! You can learn more about personalization in Chapter 9.

5. Follow-Up

What happens when your email conversion funnel sequence is done? Don't abandon people in the funnel when it's over. Instead, make sure you continue to nurture and engage them with future email campaigns and automations based on the behaviors they display on your website and when interacting with your future email messages. This is essential even if the conversion funnel ended in a sale. The relationship isn't over when someone makes a purchase. In fact, the relationship is even more important because it costs less to keep an existing customer and turn them into repeat customers and loyal brand advocates than to attract new customers.

For people who purchased products at the end of a conversion funnel, you should continue to send them your email newsletter as well as renurturing and re-engagement messages. Renurturing email funnels are used like any kind of nurturing sequence of messages. They simply continue to build a stronger relationship with subscribers who are in the middle of the marketing funnel (either because they haven't made a purchase from you, or they've already completed a purchase and aren't ready to make another one). You can create email funnels for this audience that either lead to conversions or don't. The choice is yours.

Similarly, re-engagement funnels are used to reactivate dormant customers. As such, they include a conversion. This type of email conversion funnel includes a message asking if the dormant contact still wants to be on your list. It could include a call to action that simply asks the recipient to click a button to stay on your list, or it could include a promotional offer, such as a discount on a specific product or service. If the recipient acts, they have obviously re-engaged with your brand and stay on your email marketing list.

STEPS IN AN EMAIL MARKETING CONVERSION FUNNEL

Most email marketing conversion funnels follow a proven pattern to motivate recipients to act. You can adjust the timing and order of these steps. If your offer is extremely simple, you could even eliminate some of these steps. The truth is it's easier to persuade people to take some actions than others. Therefore, people might need more persuading to do something like make a purchase or sign up for a free product demonstration than they would to download a free checklist or ebook. Following are the five primary steps in an email conversion funnel:

1. Make recipients aware of the action you want them to take.
2. Build interest in the offer by describing it and its benefits to recipients.
3. Give proof that the offer can solve recipients' problems or address their pain points.
4. Provide additional help and resources related to the offer.
5. Follow up after the action has been taken by recipients.

As mentioned previously, you can use all these steps or just some in your email conversion funnels. It's also important to note that these steps don't correlate with the number of messages you include in your sequences. Depending on the offer and audience, you could address all these steps in two, three, five, seven, or more messages. Furthermore, not everyone moves through an email funnel perfectly. Many won't complete your call to action after receiving the first message in your sequence. Those people need a different set of messages to persuade them to act than people who act immediately. Just as there are holes in your overall marketing funnel, there are holes in your email conversion funnels, too, so try to seal up as many as possible with additional messages.

EMAIL CONVERSION FUNNELS FOR ACQUIRING

The most effective email conversion type for acquisition is the lead magnet opt-in funnel. This is the sequence of messages sent after someone submits your opt-in form requesting your lead magnet. You can see an example of a comprehensive two-week lead magnet opt-in email conversion funnel sequence in Figure 8–2 on page 124. Notice if the recipient doesn't download the lead magnet after receiving the Day 1 message, there are three different messages in the sequence that address this hole in the funnel. On Days three, six, and ten, the sequence attempts to recapture recipients who have yet to act. With these special reminder messages, you have a chance to convert more people overall.

You'll learn more about writing email messages for your email marketing funnels in Chapter 10. This chapter focuses on building your funnel sequences to accomplish specific goals. However, it's important to understand that by the end of the message sequence (which would be the Day 14 message in the funnel shown in Figure 8–2), recipients should have taken your desired action and gotten more information from you that builds their relationship with your brand and sets their expectations for what kind of content they'll get from you in the future. Even if your conversion funnel wasn't built to lead to a sale, you can include sales-oriented language in the final message of the sequence. This is the perfect place to mention your product or service that is directly related to the problem or pain point addressed by your lead magnet or your sequence so far. By this point in the automation, recipients understand who you are and what your brand promises. If they've stayed with you this far, they're interested in your brand and are usually willing to learn about your highly relevant products and services without feeling like they're being spammed or subjected to an unwelcome, hard sales technique. Just be careful. You don't want to ruin all the hard work you've done so far in building recipients' trust in your brand with an over-the-top, irrelevant sales message at the end.

EMAIL CONVERSION FUNNELS FOR NURTURING

Figure 8–2 on page 124 provides an example of a conversion funnel sequence for acquisition purposes. The conversion was downloading a lead magnet. Nurturing email marketing funnels can be designed for conversions as well. For example, you could send a link to sign up for a free online course related to a topic that could move people in the middle of the funnel to the bottom where you can then create a separate email conversion funnel that promotes that related product or service as the

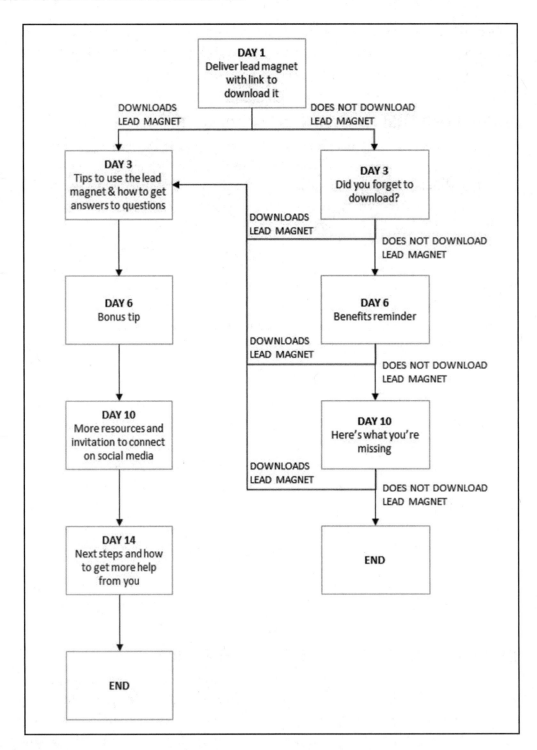

FIGURE 8–2. Example Two-Week Lead Magnet Opt-In Email
Conversion Funnel Sequence

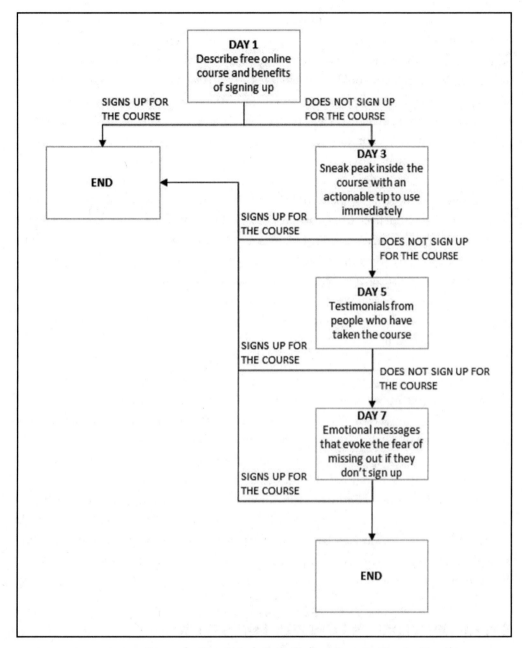

FIGURE 8–3. Example One-Week Free Online Course Opt-In Email
Conversion Funnel Sequence

natural next step after completing your free online course. Figure 8–3 shows an email
conversion funnel for a nurturing sequence that offers a free online course to move
people from the middle of the overall marketing funnel to the bottom for a services
business.

In the sequence outlined in Figure 8–3, you need to begin by explaining the course and how it will benefit your audience. You also need to include the call to action in your messages, which invites them to take the course. You can deliver the course using an online course delivery tool like Teachable (https://teachable.com), SkyPrep (https://skyprep.com), DigitalChalk (www.digitalchalk.com), or Thinkific (www.thinkific.com). If you use WordPress, there are a variety of free and premium plug-ins available that make creating online courses and offering lessons directly on your website, such as WP Courseware (https://flyplugins.com/wp-courseware), LearnDash (www.learndash.com), LearnPress (https://wordpress.org/plugins/learnpress), and Sensei (https://woocommerce.com/products/sensei). In addition, your messages should provide proof that the course will deliver what you promise in the form of testimonials and a sneak peek into what the course includes. Of course, every message should include the call to action making it easy for recipients to sign up at any time.

Note that once someone signs up for the course, a separate email autoresponder should be sent that confirms they've joined the course, provides any important instructions, and offers sources for help if they have questions. Autoresponders are one-time automated messages rather than automated sequences of messages. They are discussed in detail in Chapter 11. In addition, a follow-up email sequence should begin automatically when a person completes the course. Depending on your goals, that sequence could be information for relationship-building purposes, or it could be a new sales conversion funnel created to promote your service as the natural next step after the course is completed. An example is provided in Figure 8–4 on page 127.

The same concept applies if you're building a nurturing conversion funnel to move subscribers from the middle of the funnel to the bottom by offering a free product demonstration. Figure 8–5 on page 128 shows what this nurturing conversion funnel sequence might look like. For recipients who convert and schedule free demonstrations, they should automatically be placed into a separate sales conversion email marketing funnel where they receive a sequence of messages after their demonstrations, motivating them to purchase the product.

EMAIL CONVERSION FUNNELS FOR SELLING

Email conversion funnels for sales are created to motivate recipients to make a purchase. Continuing the example from the previous section that used a free product demonstration to move prospects closer to the bottom of the overall marketing funnel, you could follow up after the completion of that nurturing conversion funnel with a separate sales conversion funnel offering your service as the natural next step to solve the recipient's problem. Figure 8–4 on page 127 shows how that sequence could work.

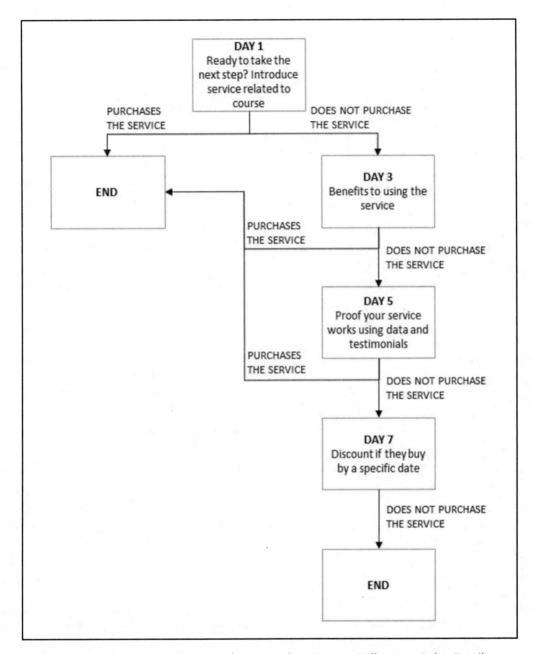

FIGURE 8–4. Example One-Week Free Online Course Follow-Up Sales Email Conversion Funnel Sequence

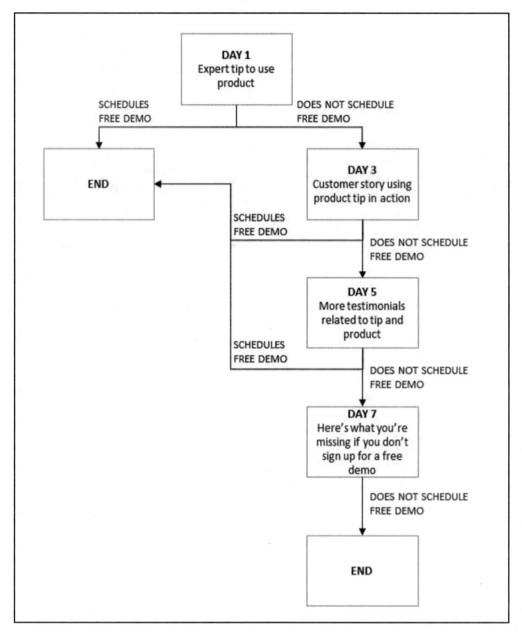

FIGURE 8–5. Example One-Week Free Product Demonstration Email Conversion Funnel Sequence

Depending on the type of services you offer, you might want to extend this sales funnel to two weeks. You could also include one more follow-up message a week after the last message is sent to people who didn't convert. Keep in mind, just because someone doesn't buy your service at the end of this conversion sequence doesn't mean you should give up. Create a follow-up conversion funnel and try to sell the service to people who didn't buy, offering different benefit messages and promotional offers, such as a new discount. By segmenting your audience between people who opened your messages the first time you sent them and those who didn't, you'll be able to target people who showed some interest in your service based on their interactions with the messages in your first sales conversion funnel. These are people who are further down your overall marketing funnel based on their actions and assumed interests, so focus on them in your follow-up email marketing efforts.

Continuing the free product demonstration example from the previous section, once someone completes a product demonstration, you can follow up with a sales conversion funnel to motivate them to purchase the product they saw in action during the demonstration. This sequence should start with a reminder of the useful features discussed during the demonstration and how those features benefit prospects. If recipients don't purchase the product, subsequent messages should be sent as reminders, and a discount can be offered to boost conversions. As discussed earlier, it's up to you if and when you decide to offer a discount based on your financial goals. You can see the message sequence for this sales conversion funnel in Figure 8–6 on page 130.

You can modify the length of this sales conversion funnel to make it shorter or longer depending on your goals. You can also introduce the special offer on your product later in the sequence or not at all. Again, the choice is yours. The important thing is to try to incent people in this conversion funnel to make a final purchase decision. At this point, you've moved them to the bottom of your overall marketing funnel, so it's important to provide just enough incentive that they'll be motivated to make that final purchase decision. However, you don't want to give up too many profits by offering discounts too early to people who would buy without them.

EMAIL CONVERSION FUNNELS FOR RENURTURING

As mentioned earlier, you shouldn't stop creating email funnels for the people on your email marketing list after they buy from you. Instead, you should continue to nurture and engage with them so they buy from you again. Figure 8–7 on page 131 shows what this process looks like visually.

Renurturing conversion funnels are part of your regular nurturing conversion funnels, but you can also create unique renurturing conversion funnels for targeted segments of your audience who have purchased specific items or taken specific actions. For example, rather than simply sending an autoresponder message that confirms a customer's purchase (discussed in Chapter 11), you can send a renurture campaign. These are particularly successful immediately following a purchase when people feel

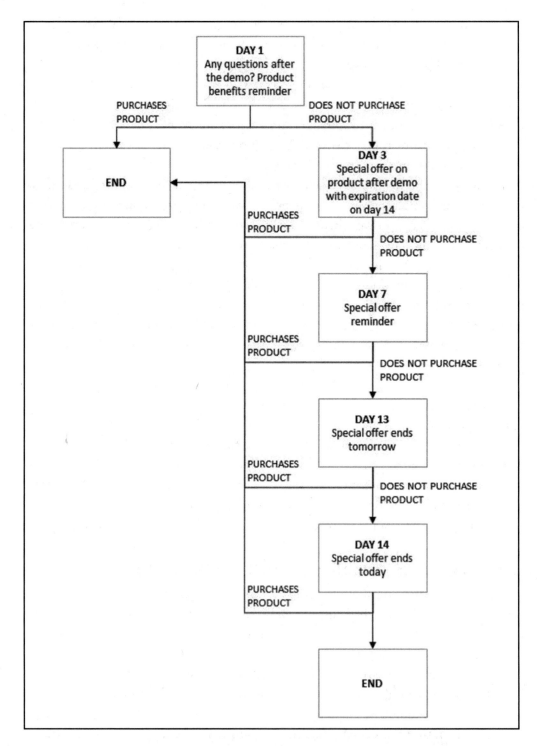

FIGURE 8–6. Example Two-Week Free Product Demonstration Follow-Up Sales Email Conversion Funnel Sequence

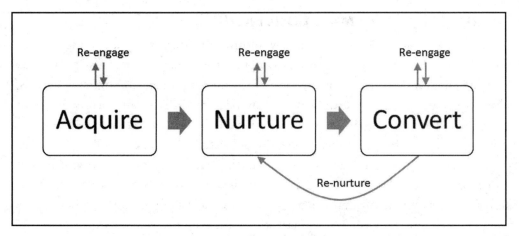

FIGURE 8–7. Email Marketing Process

good about the items they just bought. Such a campaign could include useful tips about how to use the product or a personal story. The desired conversion could encourage people to follow your brand on social media, take a survey, write a review, or share what they bought from you on their own social media profiles. None of these actions ask people to make another purchase, so they're not sales conversion funnels. Instead, each asks them to take another action that will benefit your brand by building a relationship that could lead to word-of-mouth marketing, brand loyalty, and future sales. Therefore, they are examples of a special type of nurturing conversion funnel used to renurture customers after a purchase has been made.

In addition, don't forget the people who fall out of your email marketing process. It's important to try to re-engage these inactive subscribers. Not only can inactive subscribers hurt the deliverability of your future messages overall (as you learned in Chapter 3), but they are also not helpful to you in terms of boosting sales and building your business over time. You need to try to re-engage dormant subscribers to cleanse your email list and maximize your email marketing results as well as the return on your email marketing investments. To do this, you can send re-engagement conversion funnels at all stages of the email marketing process: acquisition, nurturing, and sales conversion.

A re-engagement conversion funnel is a sequence of messages that asks recipients to take some kind of action to stay on your email list. That action might be as simple as clicking on a link to stay subscribed, or it could be to download a piece of free content or take a survey. While you don't want the action to be difficult or time-consuming, it's up to you to determine what level of engagement you need for you to invest time and money into continuing to market to them via email.

IMPROVING YOUR EMAIL CONVERSIONS

The goal of any email conversion funnel is to convert recipients by motivating them to take an action. There are three key ways to improve your email conversions. If you focus on each of these methods for boosting the performance of your email conversion funnels, your results will go up. First, track your conversion rates. You can learn more about tracking in Chapter 12. Second, make sure you're offering quality lead magnets. Go back and read Chapter 7 for a refresher on creating irresistible lead magnets. Third, segment your audience so you can deliver highly targeted, personalized content. Segmentation is discussed in detail in Chapter 9. In addition, invest in professional copywriting and design services to instantly improve prospects' perceptions of your offers, and you'll be on your way to watching your email marketing return on investment climb.

List Segmentation

Segmenting your email list can increase your message open rate by nearly 15 percent and the number of clicks on links within your messages by 60 percent, according to February 2017 statistics from MailChimp (https://mailchimp.com/resources/research/effects-of-list-segmentation-on-email-marketing-stats/). For years, research has shown that segmentation improves not just open rates and clicks but also deliverability, sales leads, transactions, revenue, and more. In other words, if you're not segmenting your email marketing list, you're losing opportunities to reach your goals.

So, what exactly does it mean to segment your list? *List segmentation* is the process of breaking your email marketing list up into smaller groups of people with similar demographic, psychographic, or behavioral traits. As you learned in Chapter 2, these traits are used by marketers to build buyer personas for the specific purpose of audience segmentation. Rather than offering everyone on your list the same thing, you can send targeted offers to specific groups of people on your list that are most likely to appeal to them.

For example, if you own a vitamin and supplements store, you probably sell some products that would appeal to senior citizens and others that would appeal to parents for their young children. You also probably sell products to help people lose weight and others to help people gain muscle mass. You could set up an email conversion funnel and send the same message to everyone on your list. That message might be about your vitamin supplement for women over the age of 55. But how many people on your list are likely to be interested in that product? Probably fewer than half. For recipients who are not interested in that product because they're not women over the age of 55 and do not shop for women over 55, they'll quickly become annoyed with your brand if they continually receive irrelevant messages from you. That means they're more likely to unsubscribe from your list, and you'll lose your ability to market to them via email in the future.

You can solve this problem by segmenting your list so you send only highly relevant messages to your subscribers. Your results will naturally be better when you send the right messages to the right people. Rather than being annoyed with your brand, they'll be happy to receive your messages because those messages include information and promotions they're interested in. For many, that's why they signed up to your list in the first place.

How you segment your email marketing list depends on a few factors. First, you're limited by the features offered by your email marketing provider. Some email marketing tools are filled with features that make it easy to segment your list in multiple ways, but other tools have fewer segmentation options. If segmentation is important to you, make sure you research the current offerings by the email marketing service providers you're considering. Remember, even if segmentation isn't important to you today, it will be in the future as your list and your business grow. Once you're more comfortable with email marketing and you realize how much your results could improve if you segmented your list, you'll wonder why you waited so long to start doing it.

> **Warning**
>
> If you're capturing visitors' behaviors and clicks, make sure your website's privacy policy explains how you collect and use that data so you're not violating any laws.

You also need to connect your website with your email marketing tool to effectively segment your list. For example, you must be able to track the actions people take on your website, such as links they click and pages they view so you can segment your list based on those behaviors. Behavioral segmentation is very effective. If you can't follow a contact's behaviors between your email messages and your website, you're missing a big opportunity. Most email marketing providers make it easy to integrate your email marketing tool with your website. Typically, all you need to do is paste some code into your website to enable tracking and integration. Check with your email service provider to get the correct instructions to complete your integration. Keep in mind, your website and email marketing tool should also be integrated with your website analytics tool, such as Google Analytics, so you can fully track and analyze your contacts' behaviors across your content and communications. With this information, you can create highly targeted email funnels for niche audiences.

HOW TO GET INFORMATION TO USE FOR SEGMENTATION

Segmentation works only if you have information to create groups of similar contacts. Some of this information is easier to get than other information. For example, you can obtain a contact's location from a shipping address in an order from your website. However, it's more difficult to get a contact's location or other demographic information if they've never purchased anything from you. Alternately, you can determine which of your products or services contacts are most interested in based on their prior purchases, the links they've clicked in your email messages, or the pages they've visited on your website. This type of information can also be inferred based on the behaviors displayed by your contacts.

What this means for all email marketers is that segmentation is an ongoing process. You'll constantly work to acquire and update demographic, psychographic, and behavioral information about the people on your email list. To that end, you need to set up processes to collect this information. That's why integrating your email marketing, website, and web analytics tool is so important. Also, you can send questionnaires to your list asking contacts to provide more information about themselves so you can better tailor content to them. People who like your brand are likely to take a few minutes to provide this information so their inboxes are filled only with relevant content. However, there are more ways to collect information for list segmentation. Some of the most commonly used tactics are described below.

Opt-In Form

The more information you ask for, the fewer opt-ins you'll get, so be careful. Don't ask for too much information or for highly personal information. Instead, ask for information like zip codes. Zip codes are a fairly nonintrusive piece of information to request, but they can be very helpful in segmenting your audience by geographic locations.

Customer Account Information

When people purchase products or services from your website, you have the chance to collect important information that you can use for segmentation. For example, collecting their address and birth date gives you valuable demographic information to leverage in future email conversion funnels.

Products Purchased

The products and services people buy on your website give you direct insight into their interests, which can be used for highly targeted email messages. Tracking this information and connecting it to contacts' profiles in your email marketing tool is one of the most effective ways to segment your list to improve future email marketing results.

Pages Visited on Your Website

If someone visits a specific product or service page on your website, it's highly likely that they have an interest in that product or service. That means you have a significant opportunity to track that information and use it in future email marketing initiatives to push them further through the middle of the marketing funnel.

Links Clicked on Your Website and in Your Emails

Just as the pages visited on your website show a person's interest in your products and services, so do links they click on within your website or email messages. Track these clicks and segment people who click on them from the rest of your email list so you can send targeted, relevant messages to them.

Lead Magnet Requests

When a person requests one of your lead magnets, you should assume they're interested in the products or services you offer that are related to the information provided in the lead magnet. As such, you should segment people who request specific lead magnets and create targeted email conversion funnels for them.

Webinars Attended

Webinars are a type of lead magnet, but they're so effective for pushing leads through the overall marketing funnel that they're listed separately here. People who attend a webinar should be segmented within your email marketing list, and they should receive relevant messages in multiple follow-up conversion funnels. Think of it this way: when someone takes the time to attend a live, one-hour webinar, they're making a commitment, and that commitment is one you can usually leverage to make a sale or at a minimum to move people closer to the bottom of the funnel.

SEGMENTATION STRATEGIES

Once you've collected data you can use for segmentation purposes, it's time to develop some strategies to boost your email marketing results. In simplest terms, there are two ways to segment your list: based on who your contacts are (demographic and psychographic traits) and on what your contacts have done (behavioral traits). In most cases, segmenting based on behaviors yields the best email marketing results, but your goal should be to develop targeted email conversion funnels based on the data you have. Remember, a key to email marketing success is testing, so experiment with your data to find the most effective targeted campaigns. "Common Email Segmentation Strategies" lists a number of popular segmentation strategies you can use to improve your own email marketing results.

Position in the Marketing Funnel

An important segmentation strategy is separating your email list by contacts' positions in your overall marketing funnel. Contacts at the top of the funnel aren't close to a purchase. They're at the earliest stages of the consumer buying cycle and need very different content from your brand than people in the middle of the funnel who are

COMMON EMAIL SEGMENTATION STRATEGIES

Demographic and Psychographic Characteristics	*Behavioral Characteristics*
Location	Position in the marketing funnel
Gender	Clicks
Birth date	Purchases
Age	Pages visited or not visited on your website
Anniversary	Lead magnets requested
Income	On-site searches
Occupation	Opened email messages
Education	Engagement dormancy
Marital status	Missing behaviors
Interests	Buyer loyalty
Hobbies	Shopping cart abandonment
Favorite website and blogs	Amount spent

in the research stage and people in the bottom who are very close to making a buying decision. Sending a free shipping offer to a consumer at the top of the funnel is unlikely to deliver conversions, but the same offer sent to consumers at the bottom of the funnel could be extremely successful. Segmenting your list and building email conversion funnels that match the content to the recipient's position in the marketing funnel is far more effective than sending a single offer to a broad audience.

Purchases

If someone purchases a specific product or service, you have an important piece of data. This purchase shows they're interested in a specific type of product or service that delivers a certain set of features and benefits. Segmenting your list so you can send messages that promote add-on products, discounts on replenishments, and other relevant offers to contacts who show interest in specific products and services is an effective strategy to increase per-customer sales.

Clicks

By tracking the links your contacts click in your email messages and on your website, you can learn valuable information about them. For example, a contact could click a link to a special promotion, which implies that contact is at the bottom of the funnel. Another small nudge through a targeted email conversion funnel could be all it takes to persuade that contact to buy. The number of times a contact clicks a link is also useful information for segmentation. If a contact clicks a link to one of your product pages on your website, your pricing page, a free trial page, a free demonstration page, or your contact page, then it's likely that the contact is very interested in your product or service. This is an opportunity to segment people who display this type of behavior and send offers that help them move beyond any final purchasing obstacles.

Pages Visited (or Not Visited) on Your Website

Just like segmenting contacts by clicks, you can also segment based on the pages on your website that your contacts visit or don't visit. If you can identify a segment of your audience who has visited a specific page, you can send them messages specifically related to those pages. Similarly, if a segment of your audience visits a page on your website that introduces a product but doesn't view important related pages such as those with tutorial videos, customer testimonials, or feature descriptions, you can target them with messages that provide this information. This type of email campaign is particularly useful for people in the middle and bottom of the funnel.

Lead Magnets Requested

Like clicks and pages visited, you can learn a lot about the people on your email marketing list based on the lead magnets they request. Keep in mind, you can use lead magnets to motivate your contacts to take different kinds of actions at all points in the buyer journey to push them further through the marketing funnel as you learned in Chapter 7. If you track all the lead magnets each contact downloads over time, you can create targeted offers and email conversion funnels to strengthen their relationships with your brand and continually push them through the marketing funnel. For example, if a segment of your email list downloads a lead magnet about a specific topic, you can continue to build your relationship with them by sending more relevant content on that topic.

Location

Location-based segmenting can be used to send local offers, promote products and services based on climate, remind contacts about time-sensitive offers using countdown clocks specific for each time zone, and more. For example, some businesses have great success sending timely promotions to national audiences during sports seasons. By segmenting their audiences, they can include references to local teams. A campaign sent during the Super Bowl or NCAA Championships could reference local teams by segmenting your list based on contacts' zip codes or states.

Gender

Depending on the type of products and services your business provides to consumers, segmenting your list by gender can be extremely effective. Not only could males and females be interested in different products or services, but they might also be interested in different features or benefits of the same products.

Birth Date

Segmenting by birth date works very well for many brands. Have you ever received an email message from a brand that says, "Happy birthday! Enjoy 20 percent off your next purchase" or something similar? The company that sent the message probably segmented its audience and sent the same message to everyone on its list with your birth date. Some companies send a message like this on the first day of every month to the segment of contacts in their email list with birthdays during that month.

Age

If you know your contacts' ages, you can create age-based segments to send targeted messages. For example, you might create email conversion funnels that offer age-appropriate products to your contacts based on their ages. You could even create special promotions for baby boomers, Generation X, and so on based on your contacts' ages.

Anniversary

No, "anniversary" doesn't refer to wedding anniversary here, although for some businesses, such as travel companies, segmenting by wedding anniversary could be very successful. In this case, "anniversary" means the anniversary of a customer's first purchase from your company. When you segment your audience by anniversary date or month, you can send special offers to each specific segment when their corresponding anniversary dates arrive. This is a great way to build a stronger relationship with prior customers that can increase brand loyalty. As a result, recipients are more likely to become more emotionally connected to your brand and buy more from you in the future.

On-Site Searches

Track the keywords your contacts use to search your website, and use that data to segment them for more successful email marketing. If someone searches for a specific product, feature, or benefit on your website, add them to a list segment made up of people who display the same behavior. You can use this information to create targeted email marketing campaigns related to that keyword or keyword phrase.

Opened Email Messages

People who open your email messages are engaged with your brand and should be segmented from people who don't engage with your messages. Further, you can segment your list by the types of messages your contacts open. People who open messages about a specific topic, type of product or service, promotion, event, and so on should be put into individual segments so you can send more targeted messages to them in the future while avoiding annoying recipients who would be less interested in those messages.

Response Frequency

How often do your contacts open your emails, click on your links, or buy from you? Each of these metrics can be used to segment your email list. The more engaged someone is with your brand, the more important it is to foster the relationship and reward those contacts. Email marketing is one of the most effective ways to build customer loyalty and repeat purchases, and since it costs less to keep customers than it does to win new ones, this type of segmentation should be a priority.

Engagement Dormancy

Just as it's important to foster a relationship with people on your email list who frequently engage with your brand, it's also important to take some time to try to re-engage dormant subscribers. Create multiple segments of your list to target different types of dormant subscribers. For example, create a segment of people who haven't opened your messages, who haven't visited your online store, and who haven't purchased anything from you in several months. Reviving relationships and winning back prior customers works very well when you can segment your audience and send those contacts highly targeted messages and offers.

Missing Behavior

What do you want people on your email marketing list to do? Your answer to that question could include many responses, such as make a purchase, visit a web page, read a blog post, and more. Don't just create list segments based on actions your subscribers take. Also, create segments based on the actions they don't take. Use missing behavior to make an additional effort to persuade inactive subscribers to take your desired actions.

Buyer Loyalty

Segmenting your audience by loyalty gives you an opportunity to not only adjust your promotions for each segment but also to modify your brand messages. Consider segmenting your audience into at least four groups: first-time buyers (people who recently purchased from you for the first time), one-time buyers (people who purchased from you one time and never purchased again), repeat buyers (people who have purchased from you more than once), and frequent buyers (people who buy based on a frequency that you choose, such as weekly or monthly). First-time buyers should get very different offers and messages than your most loyal frequent buyers. For example, it makes sense to invite the people in your frequent buyers segment to join your special loyalty rewards program. Sending this type of offer to first-time buyers or one-time buyers would not be as successful. Instead, your goal with first-time and one-time buyers should be to build brand trust and try to motivate them to buy from you again.

Shopping Cart Abandonment

Shopping cart abandonment occurs when someone selects products or services from a website to purchase online, which places those items in their online shopping cart. When the customer is done selecting items, they navigate to their shopping cart to complete their purchase transaction. If someone puts items into their online shopping cart but leaves your website without completing the purchase, then they've abandoned their shopping cart. These are very valuable prospects because they've shown so much interest in your products or services that they took the time to select those items and put them in their online shopping carts. Reaching out to these people immediately after they abandon their carts is one of the best ways to convince them to complete their purchases. However, you can also create a segment of people who have abandoned their shopping carts in the past and create targeted email conversion funnels for them in the future. For example, you can segment contacts who have abandoned their shopping carts based on the products they had selected. By reminding them of what they thought they wanted, you can evoke emotions, such as the fear of missing out. Emotions can be powerful motivators to return to your website and make a purchase.

Amount Spent

Sometimes, it makes sense to segment your email list based on the amount customers spend on purchases. This could be a dollar amount on a single purchase or on purchases over a specific period. For example, you could set a $100 threshold. When people have spent $75 dollars, you could send that segment of your audience an offer that they'll qualify for if they spend $25 more. Using this segmentation strategy, you can send messages to different segments of your audience on an ongoing basis developed specifically to reward their loyalty or thank them for making large purchases. It's a great way to build a relationship with top spenders.

Interest

You can collect interest information by analyzing the pages people visit on your website, the emails they open, the links they click, and the products they buy. However, you can also ask your contacts to provide some information about their interests to you. For example, you could send a message after someone subscribes to your email list asking them to visit an online form to set up their preferences so they only receive information that they're interested in from you. If your email marketing provider includes features that enable you to create this form, you can do so within your email marketing tool. If not, you can use a free or low-cost online form tool, such as Google Forms (www.google.com/forms/about/), Formstack (www.formstack.com/), or JotForm (www.jotform.com/) to set up the form. When people receive your message and click the link to set up their preferences, present an online form to them with a list of the topics you might send messages about. Ask the user to check the boxes for the topics they're interested in. For example, a sports store could include a list of sports, fitness activities and products, health products, and so on. Based on the items people choose, the owner could use segmentation to ensure contacts only get the messages they're most interested in receiving.

UNIQUE SEGMENTATION STRATEGIES FOR B2B COMPANIES

Many of the segmentation strategies provided so far in this chapter, such as web pages viewed and position in the funnel or sales cycle, will work well for both B2C and B2B companies. However, there are also some unique segmentation opportunities that B2B companies can leverage to increase email marketing results. A few of those strategies are discussed below.

Decision-Maker Status or Role

You can determine a contact's job title, role, or decision-maker status through information you collect via opt-in forms, sales calls, or account information after they make a purchase. Imagine you own a technology management company and you want to promote an upcoming event to your subscribers where you'll be exhibiting so they'll stop by your booth to talk with your sales team. If you segment your email list by role, you can send relevant messages to each of your contacts. For example, a message sent to someone in a decision-maker role would address some of the biggest problems they're having with their current technology management company and invite them to stop by to learn how your company can solve those problems. However, a message sent to someone in a lower-level, nondecision-making position would use very different copy. The message might invite recipients to visit your booth to learn valuable information that they can take back to their managers or directors.

Industry

Segmenting your list by industry is an important email marketing strategy that you should implement. Unless you sell products and services to companies in only one industry, your list should be segmented so you can create messages and conversion funnels targeted to specific industries. Continuing with the technology management company example provided earlier, businesses in different industries might want to hear different information about how their technology will be managed. A law firm, health-care provider, or financial company might be extremely interested in information about security while an ecommerce retailer might be most interested in support availability. A virtual company with all remote workers might be most interested in remote technology management. Clearly, if you sent a message about remote technology management to your entire list, many companies would not be interested. By segmenting your list, the right people get the right messages.

Company Size

If your customers are other businesses, then company size also works well for segmentation. Again, using the technology management company example, a large company with thousands of employees should receive different messages, offers, and content than a small business of ten or fewer employees. Something as simple as the services or products you offer or the prices you charge could be very different for large companies compared to small companies. It's best to keep these audiences separate from each other using list segmentation to maximize your email marketing results.

USING PERSONALIZATION AND DYNAMIC CONTENT

One of the best ways to improve your email marketing results even more is through personalization and the use of dynamic content. Personalization refers to editing content within your email messages for specific recipients. For example, you could use the contact's first name in the message's subject line or in the greeting of the message body. Personalization is the simplest form of creating messages for specific individuals but sending those messages in bulk (often through an automated process). You simply insert a field from the contact's record in your email marketing list into your email message. Your email marketing tool pulls that information from each contact's record when the message is sent to your chosen audience, so each message differs by that specific piece of information. Personalization works very well to improve email marketing results, but you can do even better using dynamic content.

> **Tip**
>
> Use personalization only if you're confident in the accuracy of your data. Sending a message with the wrong person's name or another inaccurate piece of information will generate many unsubscribes.

Dynamic content changes depending on the person who sees it. For email marketing, dynamic content could be an image in your message. It could be an offer, a link, or text in your message. Using dynamic content, you can create one message for your entire audience but configure that message so one or more specific elements change based on who the recipient is. For example, a clothing retailer could send a message with a 20 percent discount offer to its entire list of subscribers. However, to improve the response rate, the retailer could segment the audience by gender and make the product image in the message dynamic. Women would get a message with an image of women's clothing, and men would get a message with an image of men's clothing. When people see a message and offer that appears to be made just for them, they're far more likely to act on it.

PERSONALIZATION AND DYNAMIC CONTENT STRATEGIES

Imagine how long it would take you to send different messages to every segment of your email marketing list. The manual process could take very long, but if you're using an email marketing tool that includes dynamic content features, you can quickly create and send unique messages to multiple segments of your list. To help you get started, here are some ideas for taking personalization to the next step using dynamic content in your email marketing messages.

Similar Products or Services

You can create dynamic content based on a customer's last purchase. For example, create an email campaign that includes an image of each customer's prior purchase with a message that says, "You loved this," then show images of some related products. This is a great upsell campaign that many retailers do very well.

Pages Viewed on Website

Email campaigns with dynamic content can be triggered to start automatically when people on your list view a specific product page on your website. You can create one message and use it for multiple product pages. Just swap out the product image and possibly some text with dynamic content matched to each page.

> **Tip**
> Most email marketing providers offer personalization features, but they don't all offer dynamic content features. Do your research and choose a tool that offers dynamic content if you want to leverage it to improve your email marketing results.

Abandoned Cart

Abandoned cart messages with dynamic content that specifically reminds people what they were about to buy are extremely effective. Use copy and images that remind people of the products they wanted to purchase from your website. If they don't complete their purchase after the first message, follow up with another message that offers a discount or free shipping. With dynamic content, you can even tailor the offer based on the items in the recipient's original online shopping cart.

Gender

Whether you own a clothing store, fitness studio, restaurant, travel company, or another type of business, consider how you can segment your audience by gender and improve your email marketing results with dynamic content. Think about how men use your products or services and how those uses differ from how women use your products or services. Consider the benefits that each gender derives from your products or services. Create an email conversion funnel that uses dynamic images, copy, or offers to better appeal to each gender without having to create multiple messages.

Location

Location-based dynamic content could be as simple as displaying the closest brick-and-mortar store or office location for each recipient or including a map to the recipient's local store or office. If you own multiple brick-and-mortar locations, use dynamic content to create one message but replace special offers or contact information for each location.

Birth Date

Rather than simply modifying the recipient's birth date, why not use dynamic content to further connect your message to recipients? For example, use images and text that show recipients you know who they are and what they like. Offer a discount on a specific product they've purchased in the past (if it's one that is purchased frequently) or on a product related to something they've purchased in the past. This is a great way to build customer loyalty.

Age

Depending on the age of the people on your email marketing list, they might use your products and services differently. They might even get different benefits from your products and services. Therefore, use dynamic content to create one message, but tailor images and offers to different age ranges or groups. For example, you could customize your messages for senior citizens, adults over 40, Millennials, and so on.

Marital Status

Consider how marital status affects the ways people use your products and services as well as the types of messages that might appeal to them based on their marital status. For example, a massage studio could create an email conversion funnel offering a discount on a couple's massage for married contacts while everyone else gets a discount on an individual massage.

Parental Status

Imagine you own a furniture store, and you're having a sale. Now, imagine if you sent the same message out to everyone on your list promoting discounts on all bedroom furniture. If you've ever received a message like this, then you know the message can get very long and cluttered. Now, imagine that you send a less cluttered, more targeted message to the people on your list using dynamic content. You create one message, but to contacts who have children, you include an offer for discounts on kids' bedroom furniture while everyone else gets a discount for master bedroom furniture. You could even run an A/B split test with some parents receiving the offer on kids' furniture and others the offer on master bedroom furniture. This is a great way to determine which offer performs better before you send it to your entire list of contacts with children. When the winning offer is determined based on open rate, clickthrough rate, and even conversions (if time permits), you can send it to the rest of your contacts with children.

Weather

If you live in Florida and receive an email message from a clothing retailer in September that's filled with sweaters, boots, gloves, and winter coats, it's unlikely that you'll click through and buy anything. In fact, the message might annoy you because it's usually 95 degrees in Florida during September. The last thing Floridians are thinking about in September is down jackets. Believe it or not, I live in Florida and I get these types of messages (and print catalogs) all the time. And guess what? It annoys me. Don't the retailers look at where the people on their list live so they can send messages with products those people might actually buy at the time? It appears that many retailers do not. Don't be one of those companies. Use dynamic content to ensure the people on your list get messages about the right products at the right time. Whether it's the climate or another factor, use segmentation with dynamic content to show people the most relevant products and services in your messages, or they won't buy.

SEGMENTATION IMPROVES RELEVANCE AND RESULTS

This chapter introduced you to just some of the ways you can use segmentation, personalization, and dynamic content to improve email marketing results. Think of it this way: any time you can use segmentation, personalization, and dynamic content is an opportunity to deliver more relevant information and offers to your audience. Ultimately, that leads more people to follow your calls to action so you can meet your goals. Any way you look at it, that's a very good thing.

Chapter 10

Writing an Email Message

Writing effective email messages requires that you understand your audience, identify your goal for each message, follow email deliverability best practices, brush up on anti-spam laws, and learn some copywriting basics. A poorly written message can lead to a large number of unsubscribes and damage your brand's reputation. That's a risk no business should take. While this book focuses on using email marketing to boost conversions, this chapter provides tips you can use for all kinds of email marketing messages including both conversion and informational messages. In other words, whether an email you write will be used for direct or indirect marketing, this chapter will help you craft better messages to drive more recipients to act and/or strengthen your brand's relationship with them.

COPYWRITING TIPS AND TRICKS TO IMPROVE YOUR EMAIL MESSAGES

Before you write an email message, you should understand some copywriting basics. The simplest

Warning

Avoid using all capital letters (it feels like shouting in email messages), spam trigger words, excessive punctuation, and other items in your messages as they can raise spam flags, damage your open rates, and hurt your future email deliverability as discussed in Chapter 3.

20 COMMON SPAM TRIGGER WORDS AND PHRASES TO AVOID

1. Act now, buy now, call now	11. Make money
2. Cash	12. No obligation
3. Cheap	13. No purchase necessary
4. Click here	14. Offer
5. Deal	15. Prize
6. Earn	16. Promotion
7. Free	17. Satisfaction
8. Get paid	18. Urgent
9. Gift	19. Win
10. Guarantee	20. $$$

> **Tip**
>
> You can learn more about the 10 steps of the Copywriting Outline in *Kick-ass Copywriting in 10 Easy Steps* written by Susan Gunelius and published by Entrepreneur Press.

way to learn how to write copy for any email message or other medium is to understand what the Copywriting Outline is and how to use it. The Copywriting Outline was introduced in my book, *Kick-ass Copywriting in 10 Easy Steps*. Its purpose is to put all your thoughts in one place. Since every email marketing message you send should have a single purpose, such as one call to action that leads to your desired goal, you can use the Copywriting Outline to record all your thoughts about that purpose. When you write your corresponding email message, you can use the information in your Copywriting Outline to ensure all the copy in your message is written around that single purpose.

For an overview of the process, see "The Ten-Step Copywriting Outline" on page 151. If you consider all ten of the steps in the outline as you write your email marketing messages, you will achieve better results than if you ignored one or more of these steps. The following sections of this chapter provide more details about each of the steps.

THE TEN-STEP COPYWRITING OUTLINE

1. Exploit your product's benefits.

2. Exploit your competition's weaknesses.

3. Know your audience.

4. Communicate WIIFM (What's in it for me?).

5. Focus on "you" not "we."

6. Know your medium.

7. Avoid TMI (too much information).

8. Include a call to action.

9. CYA (cover your ass).

10. Proofread.

Step 1: Exploit Your Product's (or Service's) Benefits

If you're writing an email message with a call to action that motivates people to download a free resource, make a purchase, attend a webinar, or take advantage of a special offer, then you need to exploit the benefits of the item you're offering. Whether that item is one of the products or services you sell or it's a free ebook, if you want people to act, you need to clearly explain the benefits they'll get when they complete the action. Don't just talk about the features of what you're offering. You should clearly explain what people will get when they act. What problems will be solved or pain points addressed after that action is taken? How will acting make their lives better, easier, or happier? Will they save time? Will they reduce stress? Determine the benefits of your offer and promote them in your message.

Step 2: Exploit Your Competition's Weaknesses

If your email recipients don't act, what might they do instead? Depending on your desired call to action, it could make sense to include copy in your message that shows why taking an alternate action is a bad idea and won't deliver the same benefits as taking your desired action. Can recipients save more money if they take your action instead of a competitor's? If you can show that your offer benefits people more than other offers (including the action of doing nothing), then include copy in your message that draws attention to those differences. Never assume people know what your key benefits are or how your offer is better than competitors'. Tell them in your copy!

Step 3: Know Your Audience

Writing any email marketing message begins by understanding the audience who will receive it. You need to know the target audience who will see the message and what's most important to them. This includes not only the benefits and features of your offer that are most important to them but also the language they'll best relate to. Unless yours is a highly technical or regulated industry where very specific language is expected, your email marketing messages should be personable and conversational. Write in a language using style and words the target audience best responds to. Your message should sound like a conversation, and no one wants to have a conversation with an ad or something that sounds dull, jargon-filled, or robotic.

Step 4: Communicate WIIFM (What's in It for Me?)

No one cares about your business, products, or services. That sounds harsh, but it's true. All people care about is how your product, service, or offer can help them, make their lives better, or make them happier. Therefore, you need to write copy that clearly and repeatedly answers the question, "What's in it for me?" Expand on the benefits of your offer so recipients understand how it will affect their lives in positive ways. Don't fill your messages with information about how great your company is and how wonderful your product or service is. Instead, explain what recipients get physically and emotionally when they complete your call to action.

Step 5: Focus on "You" not "We"

As you learned in Step 4, no one cares about your business, products, or services. With that in mind, messages that focus on your business, products, or services will be less effective than messages that focus on the audience. Think about how you can word the features, benefits, and differentiators of your product, service, or offer so they talk *to* consumers and not *about* your business. An essential part of focusing on "you" rather than "we" in copywriting is to write messages in the second person. For example, rather than writing a message that says, "Download our free ebook to learn our five Facebook advertising tips," a marketing company could use copy that says, "Download your free ebook and learn five tips to boost your Facebook ad conversions." The first example focuses on the business while the second focuses on the email recipient. Simply changing your pronouns makes a big difference.

Step 6: Know Your Medium

To write effective email marketing messages, you need to understand the nuances of email communications that affect your copy. For example, email marketing messages should be structured with a main heading and subheadings as well as bulleted lists, so it's easy for recipients to quickly scan your messages and evaluate their relevancy. Email copy should be written in short paragraphs so there are no long blocks of text. It's also important to ensure your copy layout is easily readable on all devices. Furthermore, white space is important to allow readers' eyes to rest. Long email messages with a lot of copy can work well if that copy is structured effectively so it doesn't seem overwhelming to the audience.

Step 7: Avoid TMI (Too Much Information)

What information is important to your audience? Don't worry about what's important to you. Instead, think only about your audience and the purpose of your email message. All copy should speak to the audience's wants and needs. Clutter is an email message killer, so include only essential information. Use "The Red Pen Rule of Copywriting" to ensure your copy is as tight as possible. Your overall email marketing results will improve when your messages are focused and devoid of extraneous information.

Step 8: Include a Call to Action

Your call to action is arguably the second most important part of your email marketing message after the subject line. Therefore, you need to make it extremely obvious what

THE RED PEN RULE OF COPYWRITING

Once you've written your final email message copy, get out your red pen and delete at least 30 percent of it. Usually, that 30 percent of deleted copy didn't help drive your audience to act, and your overall email message will be more effective without it. Keep in mind, 30 percent isn't a requirement, but try to be aggressive in your editing and delete as much as you can. Succinct messages always work better in email marketing than messages filled with copy that doesn't directly drive recipients to follow your call to action. If you're not sure if you should delete copy, run an A/B split test with two versions of your message—one with all your copy and one with 30 percent deleted—to see which performs better. Most of the time, the winner will be the message with shorter, more succinct copy.

people should do after they read your message. Write a call to action that creates a sense of urgency and taps into your audience's emotions. You'll learn more details about how to write effective calls to action for email marketing messages later in this chapter.

Step 9: CYA (Cover Your Ass)

Before you send an email message, you should always analyze it to determine if any of the copy could get you into trouble legally or ethically. In other words, both the court of law and the court of public opinion matter, so be very careful. Be sure to include any disclaimers or proof to back up your claims so your messages and offers are as clear as possible. This could be as simple as including an expiration date and time (including time zone) for a coupon or a disclaimer clarifying that a free trial lasts only a certain number of days. The key is to leave no room for confusion, so when in doubt, consult with an attorney.

Step 10: Proofread

If you write your copy, design, and proofread your messages, you're practically guaranteed to miss simple typographical and grammatical errors. That's because you're too close to the content to see all the mistakes. It's very important that you ask another person to proofread your messages for you. You'd be surprised what you miss when you proof your own work. In addition, you can use the spellcheck and grammar-checking tools in your word-processing software or even third-party grammar and spelling tools, but don't rely on them entirely. Even tools miss errors or provide recommended edits that aren't always the best choices for your copy.

WRITING THE PARTS OF AN EMAIL MARKETING MESSAGE

Once you've learned the copywriting basics, you can strategize your email marketing message. Most email marketing messages include the same set of elements. You might not always use every element in your messages, and some of those elements might not be within the actual body text but rather in images. However, if you understand how to craft each of these parts of an email message, you'll be able to write compelling copy that drives people to complete your calls to action. When your messages land in recipients' inboxes, they have four choices: open your message, delete your message, ignore your message and do nothing, or report your message as spam. You want to aim for the first response for every campaign, or you're wasting time and money.

Subject Line

The subject line is the most important part of every email message. If your subject line doesn't capture people's attention and convince them to open your message, then you have no chance of motivating people to follow your call to action or of reaching your goals. As you write your email subject lines, keep the steps of the Copywriting Outline in mind. People are more likely to open your message if the subject line tells them how they'll benefit by taking the time out of their days to open and view the message. Therefore, focus on benefits rather than features. Use action-oriented words and phrases, and write in the second person. In addition, try to pique recipients' curiosity by promising something with an adequate perceived value.

Most important, be clear and succinct. That means you shouldn't allow creativity and cleverness to trump clarity in your subject lines. Research has shown that clear subject lines perform better than clever subject lines, so clearly tell recipients what they're going to get and briefly explain why that promise matters to them.

Consider this example. For a fitness gym, rather than sending an email with a subject line that says, "Fitness Tips from the Health Gym," the gym could use a more specific and clear subject line like "25 Proven Exercises You Can Do in Fewer than Ten Minutes Each." The first subject line is vague and talks about the business while the second subject line promises something specific that a targeted audience might be interested in. It also uses a powerful word (proven), which makes the copy even more impactful because it gives recipients peace of mind that they can trust the content in the message. Most important, the second subject line uses the second person and communicates a clear benefit—saving time—as well as an implied benefit—losing weight and getting fit and healthy.

Here's another example for a freelance writer's email marketing efforts. Rather than writing a headline that says, "Ideas for Weekly Blog Publishing," the freelancer could use copy that says, "If You're Sweating over Your Weekly Blog Posts, Here's the Solution." The first subject line promises something that sounds like it could be useful, but the second subject line is much more effective in terms of piquing recipients' interest and motivating them to click. It promises a solution to a specific problem that the freelance writer's target audience of potential business clients are likely to be interested in—how to publish enough quality blog content on a weekly basis to leverage the power of content marketing.

> **Tip**
> Visit http://ultimateguideto-emailmarket-ing.com/slw to download a free Subject Line Worksheet. Use the sample subject lines included in the worksheet or modify them to fit your business, audience, and goals.

Inbox Preview Text

The snippet of preview text that your email recipients see in their email inboxes after the subject line (if they've configured their email inboxes to show message previews) is typically between 35 to 140 characters and is pulled directly from the first lines of your message content. You can see what it looks like in Figure 10–1 below. Many people use the preview mode to get an idea of what messages are about before they open them to read in their entirety. That means the beginning of your message's body copy could help or hurt your open rate.

This small snippet of text can provide valuable information, so fill it with benefits-related copy that answers the question on all recipients' minds, "What's in it for me if I open this message?" Depending on the email marketing tool you're using, you might not be able to edit this text. However, if you can, do so. Most messages sent using email marketing tools will display text that says something like "View in a web browser" or other instructions in this preview snippet. That text doesn't help you reach your goals. Ask your email marketing provider how to edit this text, then take as much time writing it as you do writing your subject line. Also, consider how the preview text looks across all devices.

Headline

You won't use a headline in every email marketing message you send, but when you do use one, make sure it's extremely compelling. For example, if you're writing an email message that is intended to look like a personal message with plain text only, then including a headline makes little sense. You wouldn't include a headline in a personal letter, so including one in an email message instantly turns it into something more promotional and less personal. Headlines are most effective in messages with a lot of text, images, and videos that can seem cluttered without "road signs" leading recipients

SENDER	SUBJECT LINE	PREVIEW SNIPPET
Office Depot	48 Hours: Save over 55% on Premium Case Paper - Savings Coupon	SHOP NOW View in web browser Office D
Macy's	Save on fab finishing touches! - macy's Shop shoes, handbags, scarves & more. Promo code: VETS Shop Now Ca
SHOES.COM	30% OFF - Get A Head Start On The Holidays! - Plus Shop Deals For Women, Men & Kids Click here to view in you
Vera Bradley	Let us remove a few steps from your holiday home prep! - Shop 30% off your favorite styles during the Holiday S
DICK'S Sporting Goods	20% Off Your Order – Today Only! - Online Only. Plus, Free Shipping, No Minimum* Web Version Every Season Sta
Best Buy	☼ Whoa! Hundreds of Black Friday Ad deals available TODAY. - Plus, preview our Black Friday ad now. View: We
Kohl's	Save an extra 15% & go on a shopping spree. - Plus, get Kohl's Cash and shop 1-Day Doorbusters.	View this em

FIGURE 10–1. Email Inbox with Preview Text Displayed

through the message's road map. In other words, the headline and subheadings work together to guide people through your message when scanning. Most people scan messages before they read them in their entirety to confirm the messages are relevant to them. Headlines and lists used in conjunction with visual aids like images, icons, and videos can quickly confirm that the message delivers on the subject line's promise. At that point, recipients will read the rest of the copy more carefully.

A headline is like a secondary or an alternate subject line. You persuaded people to open your message with a great subject line, but now you need to use a powerful headline to convince them that they're in the right place and to keep reading. The headline should be highly relevant and follow the steps of the Copywriting Outline to ensure it communicates benefits and appeals to the target audience by speaking directly to their problems or pain points. Since your headlines need to be compelling, you should try to trigger emotions within them. When you can trigger emotions, you instantly create emotional connections between your message and recipients. Most people are motivated by emotions and most purchase decisions are made at least in part based on emotions. Therefore, craft messages that trigger emotions to boost your conversions. Some examples of emotions you can appeal to within your headline, subject line, body copy, and call to action include:

- *Fear.* The fear of missing out is powerful. No one wants to be left behind or not be able to keep up with their peers, so leverage that in your copy. For example, a subject line could say, "Only 24 Hours Left to Get 25% Off All Purchases." Time limits and countdown clocks work well to evoke this fear.
- *Trust.* Most people are risk-averse, so give them peace of mind in your copy. For example, you could include copy in your message promoting an upcoming webinar that says, "Join 1,000 people just like you who've already registered." When people know others have already purchased or registered, they're far more likely to trust what you're offering will deliver adequate value.
- *Guilt.* What does your target audience feel guilty about, and how can you alleviate that guilt? Include messages that trigger the emotion of guilt in your copy to get a better response. For example, nonprofit organizations often trigger guilt in their advertising and promotions. An email message from a charitable organization might say something like: "For the cost of one cup of coffee per day, you could help feed a starving child."
- *Envy.* The emotion of envy can drive people to act whether they're envious of other people or they want people to be envious of them. For example, an email subject line that simply asks recipients, "Do you want to be the talk of your neighborhood?" could be enough to motivate them to open the message and complete your call to action.

■ *Freedom.* The desire for freedom and the emotions it elicits can include a desire for more free time, for fewer (or easier) responsibilities, and more. Think about how you can tap into those emotions in your headline. For example, a residential cleaning company could use a headline that says, "We'll clean your house while you take the day off."

■ *Confidence.* If your target audience has a desire to be trendy or cool, and your products, services, or offer deliver a solution that can help them, appeal to those emotions in your copy. For example, a clothing retailer could use an email subject line that says, "You'll make heads turn when you wear these jeans."

Think about the goal for each of your email messages and the emotions your call to action could evoke in recipients. What are the benefits of your offer that appeal to those emotions? There are many emotional triggers and powerful words that you can leverage to appeal to those emotions in your headlines and the rest of your email marketing copy. Use them to improve your email marketing results.

Body Copy

Once you've piqued people's interest with a compelling subject line, preview text, and headline, it's time to communicate more details. For conversion email funnels, these details are about your offer. Of course, you need to continue following the ten steps of the Copywriting Outline to ensure your body copy is tailored to your target audience by focusing on the benefits that matter most to them without cluttering your message with too much information. Most important, your copy needs to deliver on the promise of your subject line or opt-in form by providing relevant supporting details.

Begin with your most powerful messages. If recipients read only the first one or two sentences of your message, you need to be confident that they'll have enough information to determine if the offer is right for them. Next, provide supporting information to tell your full story. It's important to write in the right style and use the right words for your target audience. Be conversational, and write like you're talking to one person rather than an audience of email recipients. Also, don't be afraid to break grammar rules. It's more important to sound human than it is to follow grammar rules. For example, use contractions and slang, and use sentence fragments if that's the language and style your

> **Emotional Trigger Power Words Cheat Sheet**
> Visit http://ultimateguideto-emailmarketing.com/etpw to download a free "Emotional Trigger Power Words Cheat Sheet" that you can use for inspiration as you write your own email marketing messages.

audience is comfortable with. Being personable, rather than overly corporate or robotic, can make a significant difference in the response rate.

If possible, personalize your messages and use dynamic content to offer highly targeted offers to the right people. However, don't use personalization and dynamic content unless you're confident in the accuracy of your data because personalization errors can do more harm than good. Furthermore, don't overuse personalization within your body copy. Using a person's name once or twice might seem friendly, but using their name three, four, or more times can be perceived as disingenuous. Your message should promote your offer, but it should also build trust between recipients and your brand. If the content of your message is perceived as inauthentic, people are unlikely to trust your brand, which will ultimately hurt conversions.

Of course, you need to include a description of the features of your offer within your email message, too. Benefits sell, but no one will complete your call to action if they don't know what they'll get by doing so. Don't write paragraphs and paragraphs about features. Instead, provide a concise list that briefly explains the tangible things recipients will receive if they follow your call to action. For example, include a list of chapters for an ebook or the expiration date and exclusions (if there are any) for a discount code. Brevity is key here.

For many email marketing messages, it's also helpful to include customer reviews, testimonials, customer success stories, or brief case studies to prove your claims. Anyone can claim their product will deliver a set of benefits, but when an audience can see real people who experienced the same positive results that you promote in your email message, they'll be much more likely to follow your call to action. The trick is to keep the social proof section of your email messages short. Often, email marketers will create a specific email message within a sequence of messages that is sent for the sole purpose of sharing testimonials and customer success stories. You could do the same or include one testimonial per message. Another option is to include a variation of this copy directly in your email subject line. For example, a message in your email conversion funnel offering an online course that teaches people how to make more money and sell more products by investing in Google AdWords campaigns might say, "A $10,000 Google AdWords Success Story You Can Copy." The body copy of the message would provide the details of the customer's story and tell recipients that they could experience the same results if they take your online course.

> **Tip**
> Make sure your calls to action are easy to see by setting them off in a contrasting color, a large and noticeable font, and in a separate, clickable button. If your message requires scrolling, show your call to action more than once in your message so it's always easily accessible.

The choice is yours. Even better, consider testing your message performance with and without a social proof section to see if it's helping conversions or not.

Call to Action

The call to action in your email marketing messages is critical because if it doesn't motivate recipients to act, then your investment in time and money to send that message will fail. The best calls to action are brief and clear. They explain exactly what the audience should do with no room for confusion. As such, your call to action should use action words and create a sense of urgency. Think of it this way: when do you want people to act? Do you want them to act now, a month from now, or whenever they feel like it? If you're trying to reach a goal (and every email marketing message should have a single, specific goal or purpose), then you want people to act now. By using words that create a sense of urgency like "Act now," or that create a sense of scarcity like "Hurry, this offer expires in 23 hours," people are more apt to act quickly due to the fear of missing out. Use that emotion to your advantage.

> **Call to Action Cheat Sheet**
> Visit http://ultimateguideto-emailmarket-ing.com/cta to download a free "Call to Action Cheat Sheet" filled with calls to action that you can use in your own email messages.

Your call to action should also make your audience feel like there is little or no risk involved. Instead, focus on the benefits and value they'll receive when they follow the call to action. Create a sense of anticipation and excitement, and remove any obstacles that could get in the way of completing your call to action. You want to make the process as easy as possible.

If you're including a call to action button in your message that people can click to complete the action, keep the copy on the button short. Use a powerful verb and an adverb that creates a sense of urgency, such as "now." Also, use the first person in your button copy. In this case, first person doesn't refer to you or your business. It refers to the email recipient. For example, use call to action button text that says, "I Want My Free Ebook," "Send My Checklist Now," or "Get My Coupon Code Now." This helps to personalize the action and can increase your conversion rates. You can see an example of an email message with a strong call to action in Figure 10–2 on page 161.

Footer

The footer of your website, which is the area at the bottom of a web page just like the footer of a document, is often automatically generated by your email marketing

View in your web browser

Your Free Ebook Is Here!

Thank you for subscribing to Women on Business! You can download your free ebook, *The Ultimate Guide to Land Your Dream Job*, by clicking the button below.

Your ebook includes:

- **Over 60 pages** of actionable steps you can take now!
- **Six parts** covering deciding if it's time for a new job, conducting a job search, interviewing, and starting your new job.
- **FREE Worksheet**: Job Change Self-Assessment

Download My Ebook!

FOLLOW US:

FIGURE 10–2. Email with Call to Action

provider based on information in your account. Usually, the footer includes the sender's company name, address, and phone number. It's also a good idea to add your business' website URL to the footer, as well as your social media account icons (make sure these are live links that people can click to follow you), and your logo (if it's not already in the header of your message). An unsubscribe link should also be included in the footer that offers a way for people to unsubscribe from your list in one easy step.

WRITING DIFFERENT TYPES OF EMAIL MARKETING MESSAGES

You can and should get creative in the kinds of email marketing messages you send, but most of those messages will fall into one of three primary types: one-time campaigns, automated sequences, or newsletters. Each type of message has a slightly different purpose as described in the remainder of this chapter. Once you're clear on the differences, check out Chapter 13 and the Appendix for examples and resources to access sample message swipe files that will make writing your email marketing messages even easier.

Ad Hoc or Automated One-Time Campaigns

One-time email marketing campaigns are single-message campaigns that can be sent on an ad hoc (unscheduled or as needed) basis or on an automated basis, such as autoresponder campaigns. Autoresponders are discussed in detail in Chapter 11, so this chapter focuses on ad hoc campaigns. If you want to send one promotional or informational email message to a segment of your email marketing list or your entire list, you can do so with an ad hoc campaign (often referred to as one-off campaigns). For example, a promotional ad hoc campaign could hype a new blog post or a 24-hour discount. An informational ad hoc campaign wouldn't include a *promotional* call to action. Instead, it would include useful, meaningful, and relevant information to foster a relationship with recipients that leads to brand trust, purchases, and brand loyalty over time. To write this type of message, follow the Copywriting Outline steps, be clear, be brief, and appeal to emotional triggers. Use the elements of an email marketing message included in this chapter within your body copy, and you'll be able to craft a message that your target audience will want to receive, open, read, and respond to by following your call to action.

Automated Sequences of Messages

An automated sequence of messages is also called an email marketing funnel. This book focuses on email conversion funnels, which were discussed in detail in Chapter 5. Review that chapter for a refresher on how to set up message sequences and ideas for what to include in each message within a conversion sequence. More examples are included in Chapter 13.

Newsletters

Newsletters are usually sent for informational purposes only, although they can include promotional messages. Just be careful to keep promotional messages to a minimum in your newsletters, or you're not really sending informational newsletters—you're sending promotions disguised as newsletters. Your audience won't fall for it, and they won't like it. If your newsletters turn into promotional messages, your unsubscribe rate will go up.

Newsletters are typically sent on a consistent basis, such as daily, weekly, biweekly, or monthly. You can include original content in your newsletters where you write a complete article (or multiple articles) specifically for your subscribers that aren't published or shared anywhere else. If you prefer, you can use your newsletter to send your latest blog content. Write short teaser descriptions of each of your newest blog posts and include links to each within your newsletters so recipients can click through to read the full posts on your website. Another option is to send curated content through your newsletters. To do this, you can search the web for great content that your target audience is likely to enjoy and send the links along with descriptions of each within your newsletters. You could also combine some of these types of content (original articles, linked blog posts, and curated content) in your newsletters.

Most important, avoid sending newsletters that only include information about your company. Remember, people care about how your business, products, and services can help make their lives better, easier, or happier. Your newsletter copy should be useful and meaningful to your audience and filled with far more content that prioritizes their wants and needs and significantly less content that prioritizes your company's wants and needs (which could include talking about the award you won or the retreat your team went on). It's nice to give people a glimpse behind the scenes of your company to make it seem more human, but exercise restraint and keep this type of content to a minimum.

Consider what your purpose is for sending a newsletter. Is it to build brand trust? Is it to establish yourself as an expert in your field? Is it to sell more products or services? Depending on your answers, the content you include in your newsletters could vary. As with all email marketing initiatives, identify your purpose, then craft messages (in this case, newsletters) that align with it.

IMPROVING YOUR COPY AND YOUR EMAIL MARKETING RESULTS

In email marketing, one thing is certain—everything can be and should be tested. That means all your message elements should be tested to determine what copy drives the best results. Create A/B split tests and experiment with your subject lines, preview snippets, headlines, body copy, and calls to action. Combine these efforts with testing your message design elements to find the best converting copy and design overall. Be sure to read Chapter 12 to learn more about testing and tracking the results of your email marketing messages.

Chapter 11

Autoresponder Messages

Autoresponder messages are a unique type of email message for two reasons. First, unlike the automated messages discussed in Chapter 5 (email marketing funnels), autoresponders include just one message—not a sequence of messages that are dripped over a period. Second, autoresponders can be informational or promotional. It could be argued that to truly leverage email marketing, all autoresponders have the potential to be promotional and should be used as such. However, how you use and write autoresponder messages depends on your audience as well as on what they expect and accept from your brand.

As with all your email marketing messages, keep your autoresponders focused on a single purpose and call to action whenever possible. Everything you've learned about email marketing so far in this book applies to autoresponders, too. Therefore, be clear, be brief, be interesting, be personable, and always give more than you ask for. If you're not continually offering relevant and valuable content and offers to your audience, they won't follow your calls to action, or worse, they might ignore your messages or unsubscribe from your list. Think of it this way: your relationship with your subscribers is like a friendship. You can use email marketing to build that relationship over time, but depending on the stage of that friendship, you'll speak to those friends differently. For

> **WARNING**
>
> Often, the term *autoresponder* is used to refer to one-time auto-mated messages and automated sequences of messages interchangeably. In this book, the term autoresponder refers to single messages that are automatically sent in response to a specific action. Any additional follow-up messages would be sent through separate campaigns and automated sequences.

email marketing, this affects the language you use in your messages, the topics you write about, and the offers you deliver to your subscribers. In other words, understanding who your audience is and segmenting your list is important to execute a successful autoresponder strategy.

CREATING YOUR AUTORESPONDER STRATEGY

To develop your autoresponder strategy, consider all the different actions that people could take, which could benefit from some type of follow-up from your brand. When do opportunities arise that you could leverage to strengthen your relationship through useful, meaningful content or increase sales through relevant offers? Start a spreadsheet and make a list of every action people take related to your business, as well as every interaction you have with them throughout the consumer buying cycle. Next, think about how you could send a single, automated email response after each of those actions or interactions to strengthen your relationship and build brand trust or offer something of value.

> **Autoresponder Strategy Template**
> Visit http://ultimateguideto-emailmarketing.com/ast to download a free "Autoresponder Strategy Template" you can use to prioritize your autoresponder opportunities.

Once you have your list of actions, interactions, and responses, prioritize them. Rank them based on a few factors: the added revenue they could create for your business, the increase in trust they could create with your brand, and the likelihood that recipients will want to receive each message rather than become annoyed by them. If you have trouble ranking your list, assign point values to each of the three factors listed above. You could choose a scale of one to three or one to five. Give each opportunity on your list a score for each of the three factors. Add up the total scores and rank them based on those overall scores. With that ranking completed, you now have a list of autoresponder priorities that tells you exactly which messages you should create first.

AUTORESPONDER OFFERS

Deciding what to offer in autoresponder messages depends on the audience and the action they took that triggered it. Relevance is critical in autoresponders, so the user's experience, from the action through the autoresponder message, must be consistent. In marketing, confusion is the number-one brand killer, and consistency is the first step to building a brand. This applies to your autoresponder messages as much as it does to your advertising, content marketing, and every other part of your business strategy. Here are some autoresponder ideas to help you create your own offers.

Related Products or Services

Think about when you're at the checkout counter in a local store. What do you see around you? Often, retailers fill the area near the cash register with last-minute purchase items. You can use the same technique (referred to as "cross-selling") in your autoresponder strategy. For example, after a customer purchases something from your website (or from your brick-and-mortar store if you captured the customer's email address at checkout), set up an autoresponder message that is sent out immediately. The message can be very simple using copy that says, "Don't forget," or "You might also like," and include images, brief descriptions, and links to related products or services that naturally go with the customer's original purchase. You can see an example in Figure 11–1 on page 168, which was created using a template from ActiveCampaign.

Upsell Products or Services

The best time to offer upsell products or services to customers is immediately after they've purchased the more basic version of a product or service from you. For example, a software-as-a-service (SaaS) company that offers an online software product through monthly or yearly subscriptions could create an autoresponder for customers who purchase the monthly subscription. The message would hype the benefits of switching to an annual subscription, such as a special discount or extra account features and support. You can see an example of an email message offering an upsell service in Figure 11–2 on page 169.

FIGURE 11–1. Related Products or Services Autoresponder

View in your web browser

You Got Your Email Marketing 2-Week Lead Magnet Upsell Template - Now What?

You got your Email Marketing 2-Week Lead Magnet Upsell Template a few days ago that gave you a complete 6-step email sequence template to take your list subscribers from freebie to sale. Have you tried to use it yet?

For many people, the biggest challenge they face when it comes to email marketing is getting started or moving from simple, weekly newsletters to revenue-generating email campaigns based on strategic marketing funnel development.

If you're stuck on what to do next with your email marketing, don't hesitate to contact me! I've been doing this for a long time - and for some of the biggest brands in the world. You can trust that you'll get the help you need to develop effective email marketing campaigns when we work together.

Whether you just need help **writing copy** or you need help **creating strategies, sequences, automations, lead magnets, or bonus freebies,** I can help you!

Email me directly at susan@keysplashcreative.com to get started!

Cheers,

Susan Gunelius
President & CEO
KeySplash Creative, Inc.

> I Need Help!

FOLLOW US:

FIGURE 11–2. Upsell Products or Services Autoresponder

Referral Bonuses

Autoresponders provide the perfect opportunity to generate referrals. Send an autoresponder immediately after a customer makes a purchase that offers a special discount, free item, or another bonus if the recipient refers another person to your business. Require that the referred prospect completes a very specific action so you can track referrals accurately. For example, the action could be making a purchase, downloading an ebook, subscribing to a newsletter, submitting a form, and so on.

Time-Sensitive Discount

When people are psychologically in spending mode, it's a great time to send a special offer with a time-sensitive discount. This creates a sense of urgency that motivates them to act immediately (before they forget about the offer). Make sure you add a countdown timer to your autoresponder message so it's extremely obvious that time is running out. An example of a time-sensitive autoresponder message created using a template from ActiveCampaign is shown in Figure 11–3 on page 171.

Social Media Sharing Requests with Discounts

If customers are happy about their purchases, they're more likely to want to tell their friends and family. Therefore, you should make it extremely easy for them to do so by sending an autoresponder that includes images of the products or services they bought along with social sharing buttons for each item. At a minimum, include social sharing buttons for Facebook, Twitter, and Pinterest. Keep in mind, this is free advertising for your business. You can also include a discount on a future purchase for people who share their purchases via social media.

Loyalty Rewards

When a purchase is made by repeat customers, reward them with a loyalty bonus delivered through an autoresponder message. If you're using an email marketing provider that makes it easy to integrate your online shopping cart with your email list to track these behaviors, you can quickly set up an autoresponder that can be used to thank loyal customers, make them feel special, and encourage them to buy more from you.

Review Requests

Autoresponders sent after customers make purchases offer the perfect time to ask for reviews of the products or services those customers bought. Ask them to rate your products or services as well as their shopping experiences. You can ask them to write

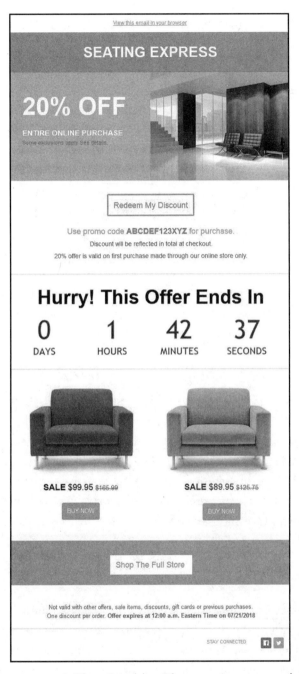

FIGURE 11–3. Time-Sensitive Discount Autoresponder

reviews on your business' page on Google or Yelp, or you can capture their reviews and publish them as testimonials on your website. Reviews provide powerful social proof that can lead directly to increased brand trust and sales among wider audiences, so ask

> **Tip**
>
> If you market yourself (a personal brand) rather than a business brand, consider asking people to write testimonials on your LinkedIn Profile.

for them. Figure 11–4 on page 173 shows an example of an email message created using a template from ActiveCampaign that requests a review.

Data Requests

You can use autoresponders to learn more about your audience for improved segmentation in future email marketing. Include a link to an easy-to-complete form within an autoresponder message that is sent after someone submits an opt-in form, makes a purchase, or performs another action. Ask them to answer one or two simple questions so you can learn more about their interests. For example, include a list of topics you might write about in your blog or a list of benefits your products offer with a checklist, and ask recipients to check the topics or benefits that matter most to them. Their responses will help you segment your audience and send more relevant content to targeted segments in the future.

Survey Requests

Autoresponders can be used to capture market research data. Include a link to an online survey that takes just a few minutes for people to complete. Ask questions about your products and services, the user experience on your website, the shopping experience, and more. Just make sure you use the data you collect to improve your business and marketing in the future, or don't bother asking for it. There are many free and affordable survey tools available, such as Google Forms (www.google.com/forms/) and SurveyMonkey (www.surveymonkey.com/) that make it easy and affordable to collect market research data from your audience.

Related Content

Use autoresponders to build relationships and trust with your audience by sending them your best content and useful resources. Just make sure the content and resources you send are relevant to them based on the actions they took to receive the autoresponder message. For example, you could send an autoresponder message that includes a link to your best blog post based on your own analysis of the content you're most proud of. Alternately, you could find your most popular content using Google Analytics or your preferred web analytics tool. If you're using Google Analytics, simply log in to your account and navigate to "behavior > site content > all pages" to see a list of all the pages published on your website sorted by "page views." Look for your relevant top posts

FIGURE 11–4. Review Request Autoresponder

and provide these links within your autoresponder message. Figure 11–5 on page 175 provides an example.

How-to Content

How-to content can be sent in an autoresponder message after someone purchases a product or service. The goal of this message is to explain tips to most effectively use the item purchased. The message could include step-by-step instructions, a tutorial video, images, and more. It could also include creative ideas about how to use the product or service that the customer might not have thought of. This technique is popular among fashion retailers that send images of various ways to wear a garment or different accessories to wear with it. The how-to content autoresponder is meant to be helpful and ensure customers get the most value from their purchases.

AUTORESPONDER TRIGGERS

There are many different autoresponder triggers you can use to establish stronger relationships with your audience and persuade them to take specific actions so you can reach your goals. Following are a variety of triggers you could leverage. Of course, this list isn't exhaustive, but it gives you a good starting point to get your creative juices flowing. For some complete autoresponder message samples you can use in your email marketing, check out Chapter 13.

Customer Service Follow-Up

What happens after someone contacts your customer service team or technical support team by phone, email, or online chat? Following up with an autoresponder message is a great way to build further trust and peace of mind with people who are experiencing problems. This type of autoresponder message should be personalized to the recipient by using their name and writing it in a friendly, conversational tone (if that style is appropriate for your audience). The message could simply say, "Just want to follow up to make sure all your questions have been answered. If you need anything else, don't hesitate to contact us at [here you'd insert your contact information]." You can even include a review request with this message or ask recipients to rate each customer service experience using a simple star rating system with one star equaling a very poor experience and five stars representing a perfect experience. If someone rates their experience very poorly, follow up with them to try to solve their problem and mend the relationship with your brand.

View in your web browser

Have You Read Your Ebook Yet?

It's been a few days since you requested your free ebook, *The Ultimate Guide to Land Your Dream Job*. Have you gotten a chance to read it yet?

To help you along your career path, here are five awesome articles written by Women on Business contributors that are filled with tips and guidance from women who've been there:

- Does Your Job Match Your Personality Type?
- 5 Ways to Invest in Your Career
- Why It's Important to Maintain Employability
- How I Created a Comfortable Work-Life Balance
- 7 Ways a Hobby Can Advance Your Career

You can find even more tips in the Career Development, Personal Development, and Job Search categories on WomenOnBusiness.com!

And for even more insights, be sure to follow Women on Business on Twitter and Facebook!

FOLLOW US:

FIGURE 11–5. Related Content Autoresponder

Confirmations

Create autoresponder messages to confirm purchases, shipping, appointments, subscriptions, and more. In other words, think of all the actions that could warrant a follow-up confirmation message. Confirmation messages won't annoy people. Instead, they provide peace of mind and help build trust. Go ahead and send them for every opportunity where they make sense. Copy in these autoresponder messages can be very informational, but if your brand personality isn't excessively formal, consider making these messages more fun than traditional confirmation messages. For example, some companies send shipping confirmation emails that say, "Woohoo! Your package is on its way!" That tone might be too informal for some businesses. A more professional message could say, "Your items have been packed with care and are on their way to you!" Include the package tracking number (if you have one), the expected delivery date, and who to contact if the package doesn't arrive in a timely manner. This is also a great place to include offers for related items—when people are excited about their recent purchase. Just add copy that says, "Since you loved [insert the item purchased here], we thought you'd like [insert a related product here with a link], too." Mention why the customer would be interested in that product by including one or two benefits with some emotional triggers described in Chapter 10, as well as an image for visual appeal. You can see an example of a confirmation autoresponder message created with an ActiveCampaign template in Figure 11–6 on page 177.

Sales Follow-Up

Any time a prospective client moves further through the sales pipeline could be an opportunity to send an autoresponder message that helps push them through the overall marketing funnel. This includes sales actions like starting a free trial, watching a demonstration, or completing a sales call. Depending on the action and your business, it might make sense to pick up the phone and call the prospect, but often, autoresponder messages are useful as sales follow-ups. For example, if someone completes a free trial of your SaaS product, set up an autoresponder message to be sent on the day the trial ends asking them to sign up or contact you with questions. Copy could say, "Your free trial ends today. Don't lose access to the awesome features you've been using to [insert problem the product solves]. Just click the 'Sign Me Up' button below so your access isn't interrupted. If you have questions or need help using [insert your product name here], contact us at [insert your contact details], or check out our step-by-step how-to videos here ['here' should link to your tutorial videos]." Of course, if you don't offer tutorial videos or have a text-only online support or learning center, you can modify the copy to reflect your business's offerings. The key is to elicit the fear of missing out

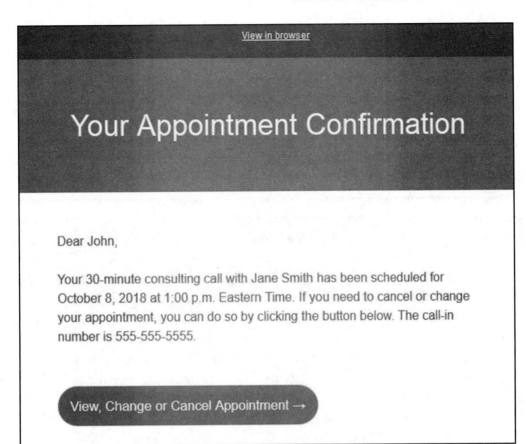

FIGURE 11–6. Confirmation Autoresponder

if recipients don't act and sign up for an account. In addition, you should remove any obstacles that might be preventing people from buying by offering easy ways to get answers to questions.

Opt-In Form Submission

Whenever someone submits an opt-in form, they should receive an autoresponder or a complete automated email sequence. For example, you can send an autoresponder message after someone downloads a lead magnet, signs up for a webinar, or subscribes to your newsletter or list. Autoresponders give you an opportunity to welcome people, thank them, confirm they're in the right place and took the right action, and provide additional information or promotional offers. When someone subscribes to your newsletter, don't just send a message that says, "Congratulations, your subscription has been confirmed." Instead, send an autoresponder message that further sets their expectations by saying, "We got your subscription request, and you'll begin to receive our newsletter next week. In the meantime, you can find tips, tricks, advice, and more on our blog. Here are links to some of our most popular articles: [include a bulleted list of your most popular blog posts that are relevant based on what each person has opted in to receive and link the post titles to the URLs]."

Thank-You Messages

Your company could send thank you messages for a variety of actions. Purchase receipts can become a type of thank-you message, or you could send a thank-you message after someone submits a review or testimonial. Thank-you messages should be used to strengthen recipients' relationships with your brand. They must be sincere, so write them like you're speaking one-on-one with the recipient. Simple is always better in thank-you messages, or you run the risk of sounding inauthentic. A simple message might say, "Thank you so much for taking the time to write such a wonderful review about [insert your company name or product name as appropriate]. We work hard every day to exceed our customers' expectations, and it's wonderful to hear that we're succeeding. I'll be sharing your review with our entire team so everyone understands how important their efforts are. We truly appreciate your business, and it's so nice to hear that you appreciate us, too!" You can shorten this copy or modify it to fit your business, but the key is to show recipients that their reviews mean something to your business and will be used to fix any problems or continue delivering on customers' expectations based on your brand promise. Of course, to send a message like the one above, you need to include a rating system or field in the review form where people can identify whether their experience was positive or negative. If you can't segment your audience between positive and negative reviews, your thank-you autoresponder triggered by a customer review submission will have to be generic enough to work for everyone. Figure 11–7 on page 179 shows an example of a thank-you message autoresponder.

Welcome Messages

Welcome messages are similar to opt-in autoresponder messages, but in this case, they're used to welcome people who joined your list without using an opt-in form. For example, they might have signed up for your list in person by filling out a form at a trade show, joining your online forum, and so on. If you acquire their email addresses outside of your opt-in forms, you should add them to your email marketing list and set up an autoresponder message to go out as soon as a contact from one of these sources is added. Of course, don't add anyone to your email marketing list unless they're aware that by providing their email addresses to you, they'll receive marketing messages. You can add this information to the sign-up form at your trade show booth or to the description

View in your web browser

Thank you for purchasing **How to Write Messages That Convert Leads into Sales**. You're on your way to learning how to create powerful marketing copy that drives results!

You can access your course materials any time by logging into the Women on Business School using the username and password that you created when you purchased the course.

Just visit http://womenonbusiness.teachable.com to start learning!

If you have any problems with your course, you can email susan@womenonbusiness.com. We try to respond to messages as quickly as possible, but please allow at least 24 hours for a response.

Thank you again for purchasing **How to Create Messages that Convert Leads into Sales**! And be sure to continue learning by following Women on Business on Twitter and Facebook!

FOLLOW US:

FIGURE 11–7. Thank-You Message Autoresponder

and rules of your online forum. Your welcome message should remind recipients how they subscribed to your list and set expectations for what kind of information they'll get from you in the future. Similar to your opt-in autoresponder messages, offer links to other useful and meaningful information, such as to your best blog posts or your online resource center.

Contact Form Submission

When someone submits a contact form on your website, make sure you immediately respond with an autoresponder message that confirms the form has been received and gives the sender a time frame for when they'll receive a response. It's a great idea to set up your contact form so people can self-select the type of help they need. To that end, include a field in your form that enables visitors to choose the reason they're contacting you. These reasons could include a sales inquiry, a technical problem, an advertising request (for online publishers), a billing question, and other. Think of the top reasons people contact your business and use them to create the list that appears in your online contact form. Create a specific autoresponder message for each reason that addresses the sender's needs.

For example, offer links to your online support center that people can refer to while they wait for a response to their technical problem, or provide a link to your online advertising rate sheet and media kit for people looking for advertising information. For the "other" reason, create a generic autoresponder message that simply says, "We received your inquiry and will be in touch within 24 hours. If you need a faster response, use our online chat tool [link the phrase 'online chat tool' to your chat window, or provide instructions to access the tool here] or call us at [insert the appropriate phone number here]." Your goal is to give people peace of mind that their form has been received, you're aware they're waiting for an answer, and you will get back to them within a specific amount of time. This autoresponder is all about setting expectations so people aren't disappointed in your response time. You can see an example in Figure 11–8 on page 181.

INTEGRATING AUTORESPONDERS INTO YOUR OVERALL EMAIL MARKETING STRATEGY

While autoresponders are sent just once, that doesn't mean they're a stand-alone marketing tactic that should run in a silo separate from the rest of your marketing plan. Instead, you should analyze each of your autoresponders to find opportunities to integrate them into your overall email marketing strategy. Two key ways to do this involve automated email sequences and segmentation. First, review each of

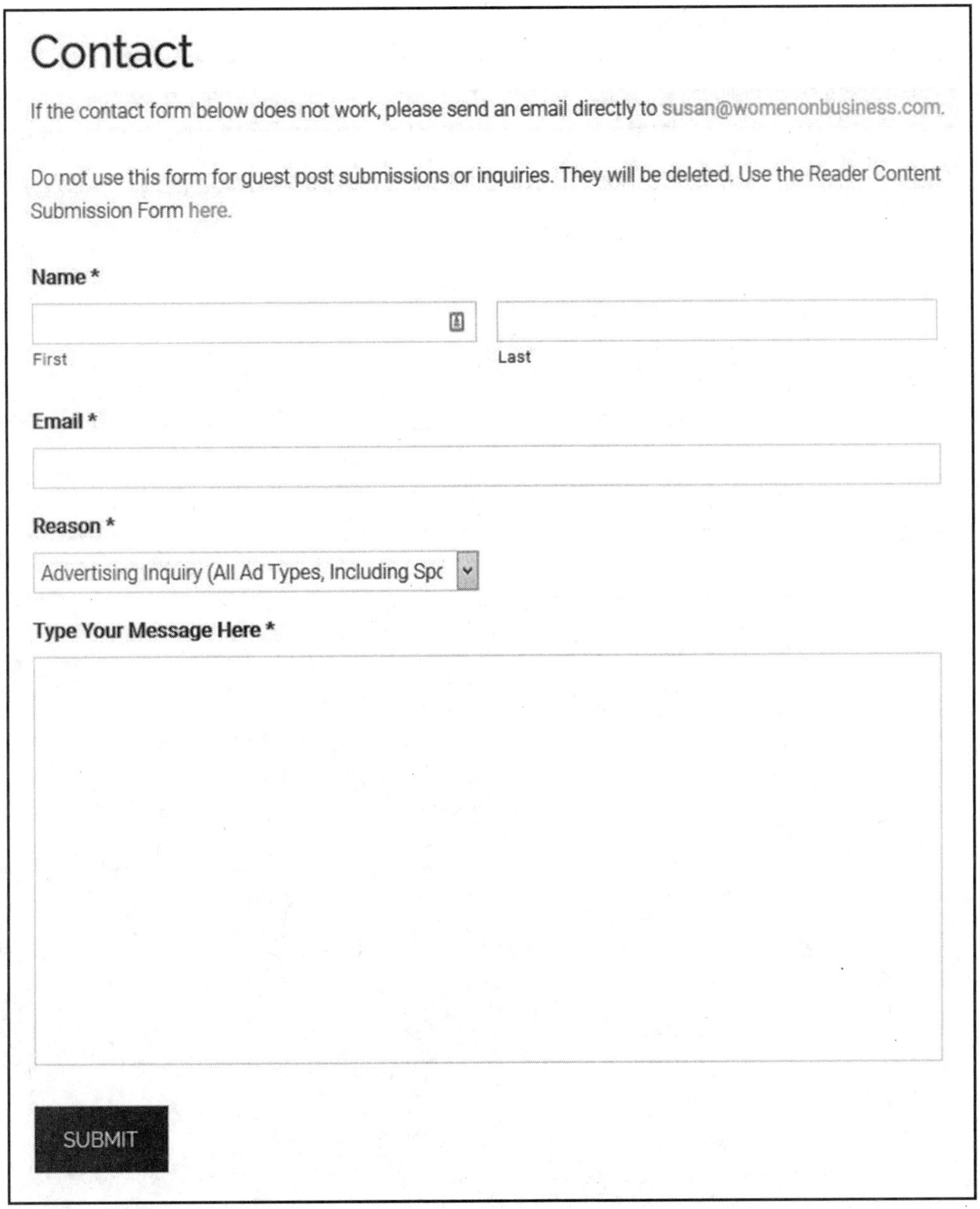

Contact

If the contact form below does not work, please send an email directly to susan@womenonbusiness.com.

Do not use this form for guest post submissions or inquiries. They will be deleted. Use the Reader Content Submission Form here.

Name *

First

Last

Email *

Reason *

Advertising Inquiry (All Ad Types, Including Spc

Type Your Message Here *

SUBMIT

FIGURE 11–8. Contact Form Submission Autoresponder Message

your autoresponders and determine which present opportunities to offer clear next steps to your audience. If there are obvious next steps, create an email conversion funnel to lead the audience through those steps and to a specific action. Second, track all the actions your audience took before and after they received each of your autoresponder messages. This is incredibly useful data that you should use for future targeting and list segmentation to improve your email marketing results. In fact, tracking your autoresponder performance is essential to improving overall email marketing performance, so move on to Chapter 12 where you can learn more about email marketing metrics and analytics.

Measuring Performance

After you spend time and money creating email campaigns, autoresponders, and automated sequences of messages, you need to determine if those messages are helping you reach your goals. Remember, every email marketing message should have a specific purpose. Therefore, you need to track the performance of your messages to ensure you've achieved your desired results. If you're not tracking your email marketing performance, then you have no idea if your efforts are helping you build your brand and increase revenue or not.

The good news is that most email marketing providers offer a wealth of data, so it's easy to track how each of your messages performs. Some of these tools even make it easy to connect your email marketing messages to your Google Analytics account or another web analytics tool. As a result, you can easily track beyond email message clicks and follow recipients' behaviors from your messages through their journeys across the pages of your website. As you venture into the world of email marketing analytics, it's best to focus on the most important metrics that every email marketer should be tracking. As you become more confident in using your email service provider's tool and your web analytics tracking tool, you can dive into deeper tracking to more precisely tie metrics to your goals.

EMAIL MARKETING TRACKING STRATEGIES

You can develop email marketing tracking strategies in many different ways. The strategy you follow depends on your business and your goals. For example, you could focus your strategy on tracking subscriber engagement, subscriber behavior, and message outcomes. Alternately, you could focus on tracking results based on where subscribers are in the overall marketing funnel—the top, middle, or bottom. Ideally, you'd use one or both of these strategies to analyze how important segments of your audience respond to your email marketing messages and how their responses affect your ability to achieve your goals.

The important thing to remember about email marketing tracking strategies is that they're meant to help you organize your analytics so you can better connect them to your business results. For example, subscriber engagement metrics support relationship-building goals as do middle-of-the-funnel metrics. The first strategy introduced in the previous paragraph tracks message results based on a message-focused view while the second strategy focuses on a buyer-journey-focused view. Of course, you can create a different strategy to find your tracking focus, but if you have a consistent strategy in place, it's much easier to compare campaigns against each other and to track trends over time.

KEY PERFORMANCE INDICATORS (KPIs)

Key performance indicators (KPIs) are measurable values that businesses and marketers use to track their progress toward meeting specific goals. As the name implies, they indicate how effectively a business is performing in terms of meeting strategic business objectives. While there are many different KPIs that you could track to determine how effective your email marketing investments are, the truth is there are a handful of KPIs that are most important to track and should be your starting point. Don't get overwhelmed by metrics. Instead, focus on the KPIs discussed in this section, and expand your analysis to more complex and advanced KPIs in the future. If you don't understand these basics, all those other KPIs won't be very helpful to you. That's because the following KPIs provide a good understanding of individual email performance, the overall health of your email list, important trends that help you identify opportunities and risks, and whether you're successfully reaching your goals.

Open Rate

Calculation: number of messages opened/number of messages sent

Open rate is one of the most commonly tracked metrics, but be careful because it doesn't always provide an accurate picture of your message's performance. Many factors can affect the open rate, such as deliverability. To be accurate, open rate should be calculated as follows: number of emails opened/number of emails delivered. However, there is rarely an easy way for email marketers to determine the true number of emails that are delivered to subscribers' inboxes. Therefore, track open rates to use for trend analysis rather than as performance indicators for individual messages. If your open rate is on an upward trend, that's a good thing. It means your content is resonating more and more with your subscribers. If your open rate is declining, then you need to improve your subject line relevance and conduct some testing to try and improve it.

Clickthrough Rate

Calculation: number of clicks on links within a message/number of messages opened

Clickthrough rate tells you the number of clicks that a message received in relation to the number of people who opened the message. While the open rate tells you if your subject line, sender name, and preview snippet text appeal to recipients, the clickthrough rate tells you if the content of the message, including the information, offer, and call to action, is interesting, useful, and meaningful enough to recipients that they took action and clicked one or more links in your message. This metric is essential to determining if your email conversion funnels are working. If people click on the link within your message to complete the call to action in an email

> **Warning**
> In all cases, accurate metrics should be calculated based on the number of email messages that are successfully delivered to people's inboxes. However, it's impossible to know this number, so you'll need to rely on the number of messages sent with the understanding that the calculation isn't perfect.

conversion funnel, then you may already have reached your goal. This is true if your goal is to persuade recipients to read a blog post or download an ebook or other piece of content. If the goal is to take advantage of a discount and make a purchase, then you'll need to connect your email conversion funnel with your website analytics tool to track recipients' behaviors on your website after they click through the email message. In some instances, you can work around this. For example, you could include a specific coupon code that recipients have to use to take advantage of the discount offer and track sales conversions based on how many people on your list used the code when making a purchase. You can see a variety of ideas to improve the open rate and clickthrough rates of your email marketing messages in "Tips to Boost Open and Clickthrough Rates" on page 186.

TIPS TO BOOST OPEN AND CLICKTHROUGH RATES

How to Increase Open Rates

- Write more effective subject lines.

- Improve the relevance of your content as described in your subject line and preview snippet.

- Change the sender name.

- Change the time when you send messages.

- Change the frequency of your messages.

- Improve your list segmentation.

- Ensure you're not using spam triggers.

How to Increase Clickthrough Rates

- Send more relevant offers.

- Improve your message copywriting with better headlines and body copy.

- Create a more powerful, clear, and urgent call to action.

- Improve the readability of your messages through better design and device optimization.

- Test using images and video.

- Ensure links are easy to see.

- Improve your list segmentation.

Website Traffic

How much traffic do your email messages send to your website? It's important to determine where traffic to your website comes from, and this includes your own email marketing messages. Again, connect your email marketing tool with your web analytics tool to track not just the page subscribers end up on after clicking on links within your email marketing messages but also the additional pages they visit and how long they stay on your site. This requires that you create unique tracking URLs for your email links that your web analytics tool can identify. These behaviors are perfect to use as triggers for future email conversion funnels and for segmentation purposes.

Conversion Rate (Including Sales and Profitability)

Calculation: number of people who completed the desired action/number of emails sent

If your goal for an email marketing message is to drive a specific conversion—such as downloading an ebook, signing up for a webinar, starting a free trial, scheduling a free demo, or making a purchase—you should track whether the message was successful in making that conversion happen. Depending on the conversion you're tracking, you might have to integrate your email marketing tool with your web analytics tool first. To determine if your email messages are generating conversions, you need to track the conversions that resulted from each individual email message. For example, you could calculate the average revenue generated per message sent in a specific campaign by dividing the total revenue generated by the number of messages sent.

> **Tip**
> The process to connect your email marketing tool with your web analytics tool varies by provider. Review the help documentation for your email marketing tool and web analytics tool to configure your integrations correctly.

To determine the profitability of the campaign, you can subtract the cost of the campaign and cost of goods sold from the total revenue generated from the campaign and divide that result by the number of messages sent. Finally, to determine a campaign's overall ROI, subtract the cost of the campaign from the amount of money generated from the campaign through sales and divide the result by the total cost of the campaign. Multiply that result by 100, and you'll determine the overall ROI.

Another popular conversion metric to track is lead-to-conversion rate. This metric shows you how well you're doing at converting people in the middle and bottom of your overall marketing funnel into customers. In this case, you'd need to make sure you're tracking only subscribers who have been segmented as being in the middle or bottom of the funnel and received the email message you're tracking. Divide the number of those people who completed your call to action by the number of people who received your message.

Unsubscribe Rate

Calculation: number of contacts who unsubscribed from your list using the unsubscribe link in your message/number of messages sent

Unsubscribe rate (or opt-out rate) tells you the total number of people who have unsubscribed from your list because they no longer want to receive email messages from you. While the unsubscribe rate is an important metric to track, be careful because it's not entirely accurate. While the metric is intended to give you an idea of how healthy your email marketing list is, it doesn't necessarily reflect a true picture. For example, many people will become disengaged with your messages rather than take the effort to unsubscribe. That means you're probably wasting your time and money sending messages to them that they'll never open. You can use the unsubscribe rate to analyze your list performance over time and identify any upward or downward trends that could indicate there is a problem with your content. However, you should also track engagement by analyzing how people interact with your messages (open rate and clickthrough rate) rather than relying entirely on the unsubscribe rate to make decisions.

Bounce Rate

Calculation: number of messages that delivered hard or soft bounces/number of messages sent

Bounce rate represents the percentage of subscribers who did not receive your email message because the email address delivered a hard or soft bounce. As you'll recall from Chapter 3, a *hard bounce* is delivered when an email address is permanently broken, meaning your message will never be delivered to it. A *soft bounce* is delivered when something is temporarily wrong with an email address, which could be fixed in the future. Bounced messages can negatively affect your overall email deliverability rate, so it's critical that you cleanse your email list and remove problematic addresses. Many email service providers take care of this for you, so check with your provider to determine whether you need to cleanse bounced email addresses from your list.

List Growth Rate

Calculation: ([number of new subscribers – (number of unsubscribes + number of bounced email addresses removed from your list)]/number of email addresses on your list) x 100

You can track the growth rate of your email marketing list using the calculation above. One of your overall email marketing goals should be to grow your email list so you can extend your reach and put your offers in front of more of the right people on an ongoing basis. If you're not actively growing your list, then your list and reach will naturally become smaller over time through unsubscribes, dormant accounts, and bounces. That means you'll lose opportunities to build relationships that turn into sales and convert subscribers into buyers. If you see your list growth rate numbers deteriorating, increase your lead generation activities as discussed in Chapters 6 and 7.

TESTING YOUR EMAIL MESSAGES TO IMPROVE PERFORMANCE

In an ideal world, you would test every element of your email messages to find the perfect ones that deliver the best results. Unfortunately, you're probably facing time and budget constraints that make testing everything for every email message impractical. That's fine. By testing some key elements, you'll be able to improve your email marketing results. Furthermore, while it can be tempting to test every message, focus on those messages that would deliver the biggest impact to your business if they performed better. These messages should be your top priorities for testing.

A/B Split Testing

As introduced in Chapter 4, A/B split testing is the most popular method of testing email marketing messages to create optimal performing messages. With A/B testing, you test one variable in your message at a time. The original message is your control message. You send your control message to a portion of your audience and send the second version with one element changed to another portion of your audience. The version that delivers better results is the winner. Here's an example:

1. You create a message inviting subscribers to sign up for your upcoming webinar. This is your control message.
2. You create a second version of the message with a different subject line, but everything else matches the control message. This is your test message.
3. You send 10 percent of your audience the control message and 10 percent the test message.
4. After 48 hours, you review the results of your test and identify the winning message based on the open rate, the clickthrough rate, or the metric of your choice.
5. You send the winning message to the remaining 80 percent of your audience.

By following the above steps, 80 percent of your audience will receive the better-performing version of your message, so your overall campaign results should be higher than they would have been if you sent the original message to your entire list. You can perform as many A/B tests as you want. If you send the same message on an ongoing basis (such as your weekly newsletter), you can A/B split test a different element each time you send it. You'll find a list of many different elements you can test to improve the results of your email marketing in "20 Email Message Elements You Can Test to Improve Results" on page 190.

Timing

Many studies have been conducted to identify the best time to send email marketing messages with a variety of different results. The truth is there are simply too many

20 EMAIL MESSAGE ELEMENTS YOU CAN TEST TO IMPROVE RESULTS

1. Colors
2. Typeface
3. Font size
4. Button size
5. Button placement
6. Call to action offer
7. Call to action text and/or design
8. Subject line
9. Sender name
10. Inbox preview snippet
11. Message layout
12. Images
13. Videos
14. Paragraphs vs. lists
15. Headline copy
16. Text only or more elaborate design
17. Time sent
18. Length of message
19. Message tone (humorous, friendly, professional, etc.)
20. Testimonials

variables at play to identify a single optimum day and time to send all your email marketing messages. The perfect day and time depend on the audience, the offer, and more. However, researchers have come up with some generalities that can help you pick days and times to send your messages that should deliver better results than others.

Most research studies identify Tuesday as the best day of the week to send email marketing messages, followed by Thursday, then Wednesday. Keep in mind, depending on your business and audience, you just might see high open rates on Saturdays and Sundays. Since these are the days of the week when the fewest email messages are sent, it makes sense that they could provide a unique opportunity for the right brands and offers. This is something you'll need to test to see if it's a strategy that will work for you.

The time of day to send email marketing messages to get the best results varies based on studies from different companies, but a few times stand out as performing better than others. Messages sent at 10 A.M., followed by 11 A.M. consistently perform well. Another opportunity to get higher open and clickthrough rates is 8 P.M. to midnight. Two other times that are worth testing are 2 P.M. and 6 A.M., but keep in mind, all are time-zone sensitive. That means simply sending a message at 10 A.M. in your time zone but not configuring it to go out at 10 A.M. in each recipient's individual time zone won't deliver the same results that configuring your message to go out at 10 A.M. based on recipients' time zones will. Of course, to do this type of configuration, you need to know what time zone each of your contacts lives in. If you have this information, leverage it and set up your messages accordingly. If you don't have this information, don't worry. You can create a special email campaign to ask your recipients for this information if you'd like to capture it for future email marketing initiatives.

CONNECTING YOUR RESULTS WITH YOUR GOALS

Remember, every email message you send should have a single purpose or goal. You can connect your email marketing results with your goals using the various metrics discussed in this chapter. Therefore, start tracking the results of each message in every email campaign, autoresponder, and automated sequence that you send. When you can see what's working well on paper and identify what needs to be fixed, you'll find that you're better able to reach your goals and improve your email marketing over time.

> **Email Marketing Results Worksheet**
> Visit www.ultimateguideto-emailmarketing.com/emrw to download a free "Email Marketing Results Worksheet" that you can use to track the performance of your email marketing messages.

Chapter 13

Handy Resources and Swipe Files

Throughout this book, you've been introduced to a variety of concepts to develop successful email marketing campaigns, autoresponders, and automated sequences. To make it easy for you to find all these resources and more, everything is included in Chapter 13 and the appendix. Here you'll find a variety of worksheets, checklists, templates, sequences, and message copy that you can use for inspiration. When resources are available for download, the direct download link is included. Also, the copy for all the sample messages in this chapter and in the appendix can be downloaded in their entirety as a swipe file at http://ultimateguidetoemailmarketing.com/sf, so you can simply copy and paste the content into your own email messages. It can't get easier than that.

LINKS TO SOFTWARE AND RESOURCES MENTIONED IN CHAPTERS 1 TO 12 (AND MORE)

All the software, tools, and resources mentioned in this book are listed in the appendix. In addition, I've included more resources in the list that will help you continue learning about email marketing and implementing strategies and tactics that will help you reach your goals. As I mentioned earlier in this book, email marketing resources change constantly. To see a current version of this list, as well as more useful marketing tools and resources, visit http://ultimateguidetoemailmarketing.com/resources.

LIMITED-TIME OFFER PROMOTION SEQUENCE

The sequence in Figure 13–1 (on page 195) could be used to promote any type of limited-time offer to your email list. For example, it's the perfect sequence to use when you're promoting a discount offer. This sequence is set up so messages are delivered over a one-week period, which makes it most appropriate for products and services where customers' purchase decisions don't take very long. Of course, you can extend this sequence by adding more days between messages or adding more messages to the series so it best matches your audience and offer.

In-Person Event Promotion Sequence

If you hold in-person events for your business, either at your location or at a separate location, you can use the sequence in Figure 13–2 (on page 196) to promote your events, invite people on your email list to attend, and send reminder messages as the date of an event approaches. Depending on where you're holding your event and if you're charging for tickets, you might need to tweak this sequence, but the basic flow works for most events.

AUTOMATED EMAIL MESSAGE SEQUENCES COPY SAMPLES

Sample Message Copy

You can download a swipe file of all the sample message copy included in this chapter at http://ultimateguidetoemail-marketing.com/sf.

This section includes sample message copy for several different automated email sequences that you can set up to market your business, brand, products, and services. Note that each message should include a personalized greeting whenever possible as well as an appropriate closing and your signature block so recipients know who the message came from. This helps to make your business seem more human and trustworthy in recipients' minds. Similarly, you should end each message with a brand-appropriate closing and a signature block using a real person's name. Be sure to replace the text in brackets with your own copy, and for sample text that is underlined, add active URL links for your appropriate web pages before you send your messages.

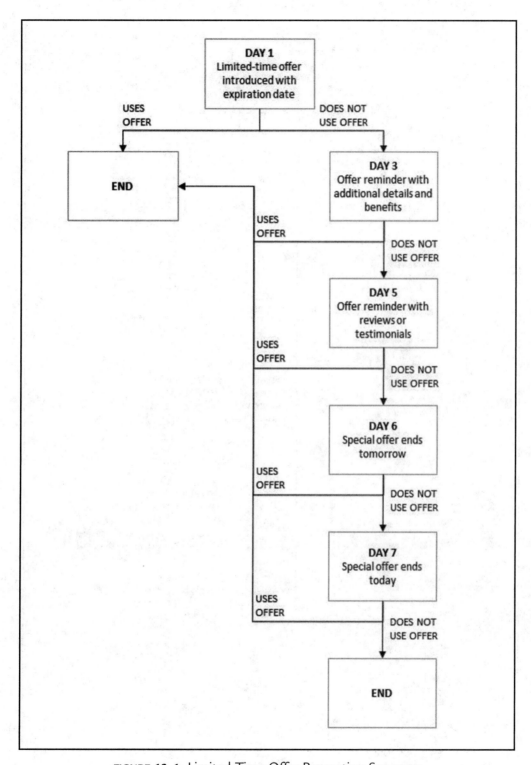

FIGURE 13–1. Limited-Time Offer Promotion Sequence

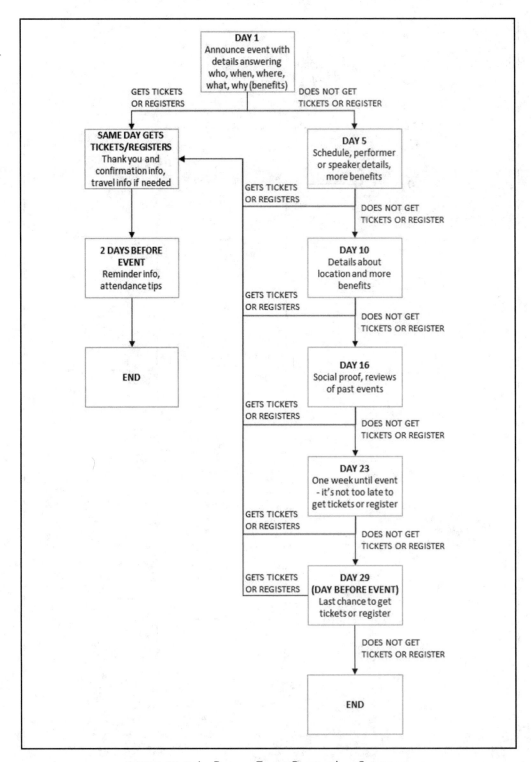

FIGURE 13–2. In-Person Event Promotion Sequence

Simple Ebook Delivery Message Sequence

This email message sequence copy has been written for an ebook delivery, but it could easily be used with some tweaks for a variety of lead magnets.

Email Message #1

SUBJECT LINE: Here's Your [ebook topic] Ebook

The ebook you requested, [insert ebook title], is ready for you! Just click the "Download My Ebook" link below to access it now. I know once you read it, you'll [insert a benefit or a problem the ebook solves].

Download My Ebook

This free ebook gives you the information you need to [insert a benefit the ebook provides to readers] **so you can** [insert a goal readers can achieve by reading the ebook].

If you have questions as you read the ebook, don't hesitate to contact me at [insert your contact information]. In the meantime, happy reading!

Email Message #2

SUBJECT LINE: You Have Your Ebook, What's Next?

Have you started reading your ebook yet? Are you already done reading it? Whether or not you've read it cover to cover yet, I'm sure you're asking a very specific question, "What's next?" Don't worry. I've got you covered.

[Insert ebook name] **teaches you** [insert one or two key things the ebook teaches readers]. **Your next steps are simple. Just** [insert the next one or two things readers should do after they read your ebook]. **Once you've completed those steps, you'll be well on your way to** [insert reader's goal or an explanation of the problem the ebook solves].

Need more help? I'm here if you need me, so contact me any time at [insert your contact information]. **You can also learn more on** [insert other resources you offer with each item linking to its corresponding URL, such as "<u>our blog</u>" and "<u>our online knowledgebase</u>"]. **I promise the team at** [insert company name] **has the knowledge and tools to help you** [insert reader's goal]!

Email Message #3

SUBJECT LINE: Where Do You Go from Here?

This is the last message I'll send you about your ebook, [insert ebook title], but don't worry. I won't disappear! You'll still receive our [insert frequency, such as weekly or monthly] newsletter and updates, and of course, you can read our <u>blog</u> and follow us on <u>Facebook</u> and <u>Twitter</u> [include any other social media channels you're active on here with links to your profiles/pages for people to follow] for useful posts and conversations.

If you're ready to take the next step beyond learning and take action, I can help you. Just contact me at [insert your contact information] and let's work together!

Ebook Delivery with Bonus Messages for Upsell Sequence

As with the preceding simple ebook delivery message sequence, the messages in this sequence could be used to deliver a variety of lead magnets in addition to an ebook.

Email Message #1

SUBJECT LINE: Here's the Ebook You Requested about [insert ebook topic]

Are you ready to [insert benefit readers get from the ebook, such as to stop wasting time or money on something]? You can learn how to do it right now by clicking on the link below to download your free ebook, [insert ebook name].

<u>Download My Ebook</u>

This ebook is filled with over/nearly [insert number of pages or chapters—whichever would be perceived as more] pages/chapters filled with tips, tricks, and warnings to help you [insert problem the ebook solves or benefit it delivers].

Your Free Bonus Is Coming!

To help you [insert benefit of ebook or problem it solves related to the free bonus item you'll give them in message #2], I'm sending you a free bonus item in a couple of days.

Watch your email for your free [insert name or description of free bonus item, which could be something like a checklist or worksheet], which you can use to [insert description of how the free bonus item will help them—make sure it's relevant to the ebook topic].

In the meantime, download your ebook and start reading. I promise when you implement the recommendations included in this ebook, you'll [insert something readers will achieve by reading the ebook that matters to them].

Email Message #2

SUBJECT LINE: Your Free [insert free bonus item title] Bonus Is Here

Have you started reading [insert ebook title] yet? If not, what are you waiting for? Every day you wait to implement the tips included in the ebook equates to [insert what readers lose or can't get if they don't use the tips in the ebook, such as money lost, more wasted time, etc.].

Your Free [insert bonus item name]

As promised, here is your free [insert bonus item name], which you can get right now by clicking the Download My [insert bonus item name] link below.

Download My [insert bonus item name]

The [insert bonus item name] helps you [explain one or two things that the bonus item can help recipients do].

Stay Tuned Because More Is on the Way

Watch your email because I'm sending something else to you that you don't want to miss!

Email Message #3

SUBJECT LINE: Have You Used Your [insert first bonus item name]?

I hope you've finished reading [insert ebook title], and you've already had a chance to use your [insert first bonus item name]. I'd love to hear what you've found most helpful so far. Send me an email at [insert email address] or post a message on the [insert company or brand name] Facebook Page and let me know!

A Second Free Bonus Is Coming Soon!

To make it even easier for you to [insert the key thing the ebook helps readers accomplish or achieve], I'm sending you a second free bonus in a couple of days.

Watch your email for a free [insert second bonus item name]. Trust me—you don't want to miss this important resource!

Of course, if you have questions or need help at any time, don't hesitate to contact me at [insert your contact information].

Email Message #4

SUBJECT LINE: Here Is Your Free [insert second bonus item name]

Your second free bonus is here! This [insert second bonus item name] is filled with [insert what features the bonus includes] and will help you [insert what benefits the second bonus helps recipients accomplish or achieve]. Just click on the <u>Download My</u> [insert second bonus item name] link below to get it now.

<u>Download My</u> [insert second bonus item name]

As you dive deeper into [insert topic of ebook that the reader is learning about], you're likely to have questions and might even want help getting things right. I'm always available to help you [insert what you can help recipients with], so don't hesitate to contact me at [insert contact information].

Email Message #5

SUBJECT LINE: Next Steps to [insert something recipients are trying to do that's related to your ebook topic and the product or service you're trying to sell in this message]

You already took the first step to [insert the pain point or problem readers are trying to solve by reading your ebook] by reading [insert ebook title] and using your [insert first bonus item name] and [insert second bonus item name]. What's next?

If you want to [insert reader's goal that your product or service can help them achieve], you need to keep learning or [insert "hire professionals to help you" if you're trying to sell a service or insert "invest in insert product]" if you're trying to sell a product. [Insert company or brand name] offers a variety of resources that can help you get started, including our <u>blog</u>, <u>Facebook Page</u>, and <u>Twitter Profile</u> [if you offer other resources, such as an online learning center or other social media channels, include them in this sentence and link each item to its corresponding URL]. However, if you're ready to take the next step by [insert "getting professional help" or "purchasing insert product name]"], then [insert company name] can help you right now.

[Insert a sentence or two explaining what your product or service is and include a list of three to five benefits that the product or service will immediately deliver to recipients].

Don't Wait Any Longer to [insert what your product or service can help recipients do, such as "Close More Sales" or "Reduce Your Stress" or "Look Your Best" or "Make More Money"]!

Are you ready to take the next step? [Insert instructions to take the next step, which could be clicking a link to buy the product on your website, scheduling an appointment, calling or emailing you to learn more, etc.].

As always, I'm here if you have any questions, so contact me at [insert contact information], **and I'll help you** [insert the problem you can help them solve or the goal you can help them achieve].

Warm Lead Follow-Up Message Sequence

The copy in the following message sequence was written as if it comes from a salesperson and with a software-as-a-service (SaaS) company in mind, but you can tweak the words and offers to best match your business, sales process, and goals. Make sure the sender's complete contact information is included in the email signature block in every message in this sequence so it's always easy for recipients to get in touch with them.

Email Message #1

SUBJECT LINE: Here's the Information You Requested for Your [insert lead's type of business]

Thank you so much for your interest in [insert your company name]. I wanted to take a moment to introduce myself. My name is [insert salesperson's or sender's name], and I'm available to answer any questions you have about [insert product or service name].

You can learn more about [insert product name] by visiting our website at [insert the URL for your product's page], but don't hesitate to send me an email or give me a call directly if you have any questions.

Thank you again for your interest, and remember, I'm here if you need me.

Email Message #2

SUBJECT LINE: Help for Your [insert lead's type of business]

I haven't heard from you since I sent my last message, so I wanted to check in to see if you have any questions I can answer. Also, I'm happy to schedule a free demonstration of [insert product name] with you so I can walk you through some of the ways it can help you [insert a problem the product can solve for the lead] and [insert a benefit of the product or a second problem the product can solve for the lead].

[Insert your company name] has helped a lot of businesses like yours, and I know we can help you, too. I'm available to answer any questions that you have, so feel free to respond to this email or give me a call at any time.

Email Message #3

SUBJECT LINE: Ready to Schedule Your Free Demo?

I wanted to touch base with you again to learn what it would take to convince you to walk through a demonstration of [insert your product name] with me so you can see what it can do and how it can help you. How does your calendar look this week or next week?

I'm certain [insert your product name] can help you, your business, and your customers. Give me a call or send me an email to set up a demo so I can prove it to you!

Email Message #4

SUBJECT LINE: What's Holding You Back?

It's been a while since you first expressed interest in [insert product name], so I'm touching base with you one more time to find out if there is any information I can provide that will help you make the decision to add [insert product name] to your business.

Send me an email and let me know what's holding you back from giving it a try. Your feedback is important to us as we work to build the best [insert type of product] possible.

Webinar Sign-Up Message Sequence

If you want to hold a webinar and plan to invite the people on your email list to attend, then you need an automated email sequence to send the invitation, as well as follow-up messages to people who don't sign up right away. Keep in mind, webinars are most successful when you advertise a free lead magnet that is directly related to your webinar topic and the product you hope to sell to attendees. Use the lead magnet to fill up your email list with people who are interested in your topic, then follow up with your webinar invitation sequence. Also, the copy in the messages in this sequence is written for a live webinar, but with some minor edits, it could be used for prerecorded webinars, too.

Email Message #1

SUBJECT LINE: Free Webinar: [insert webinar name here]

Are you having trouble figuring out how to [insert what your webinar will teach attendees]? If you're like many people, you'll continue to struggle with average (or worse, below average) results and accept that's the best you can do. However, I'm here to tell you that's not good enough for you! You deserve better.

I'm revealing exactly how I [insert what your webinar will teach attendees] in my upcoming free webinar. Join me live at [insert time including time zone] on [insert date], and I'll share my exact system so you can get the best results possible.

Click Here to Sign Up

During this live one-hour webinar, I'll show you step-by-step how you can:

· [insert something you'll teach, including how it benefits attendees]

· [insert something you'll teach, including how it benefits attendees]

· [insert something you'll teach, including how it benefits attendees]

· [insert more things you'll teach—you can include up to five things so you don't overwhelm people or make it seem unrealistic that you can cover everything in one hour]

If you want to [insert the goal people will be able to achieve after attending the webinar], then this webinar is for you. Keep in mind, there are limited seats in this live webinar, so sign up now and claim your spot!

Email Message #2

SUBJECT LINE: How to [insert one key thing people will learn in your webinar]

When I first started [insert the topic of your webinar—the main thing you'll be teaching], I made a lot of mistakes. I don't want you to make the same mistakes. In fact, I want to remove as many obstacles for you as possible so you're successful faster. That's why I'm inviting you to my upcoming live webinar, [insert webinar title].

In just one hour at [insert time including time zone] on [insert date], I'll teach you how to [insert what you'll teach in the webinar] in an easy-to-follow way. You'll leave with clear steps to put what you learned into action.

Click Here to Reserve Your Spot

To give you an idea of what I'm going to reveal to you in this webinar, here's a sneak peek of some of the topics I'll cover:

[insert a bulleted list of topics you'll talk about using phrasing like "How to . . .," "Why you should . . .," "When to . . .," and so on]

[use as many bullets as you need for your list—this should be comprehensive, but if your list gets to be more than seven bulleted items, consider combining some so it's not overwhelming]

Free Bonus If You Attend the Live Webinar

Not only will you learn exactly how I [insert the topic of the webinar] to [insert the key benefit to learning what's discussed in the webinar], but I'll also give you a free [insert free bonus item name] at the end of the webinar. Make sure you stay online until the end of the webinar so you don't miss it!

Sign Up to Attend the Free Webinar

Seats are filling fast, so click the sign-up link above to reserve your spot now.

Email Message #3

SUBJECT LINE: Time Is Running Out to Join the Free [insert webinar title] Webinar

I know you're busy, but I don't want you to miss the opportunity to attend my upcoming live webinar, [insert webinar title], where you'll learn how to [insert a key thing or two things they'll learn]. If you want to [insert attendees' top goal related to the webinar, such as "build your business" or "increase sales from your online advertising investments"], then you really need to attend this webinar because I'm going to tell you exactly how to do it.

That's right. I'm sharing my proven system to [insert what attendees will learn], but you have to be at the webinar to learn it! Just click the "Register for the Free Webinar" link below to reserve your spot.

<u>Register for the Free Webinar</u>

Seats for this live webinar are almost filled, so don't delay. Click the link above to register, or you won't learn my system to [insert what attendees will learn] or get the free [insert bonus item title] as a bonus.

If you're serious about [insert attendees' primary goal or the top benefit they want to receive from the webinar], then it's time to do something about it! <u>Register for my free [insert webinar title] webinar now</u> and take the first step.

SINGLE MESSAGE EMAIL COPY SAMPLES

The remainder of this chapter includes a variety of copy samples you can use to get ideas for your own messages. Every message is included in a swipe file that you can download at http://ultimateguidetoemailmarketing.com/sf, so it will be easy for you to copy and paste the text directly into your own email marketing campaigns and autoresponders. Keep in mind, you should start each message with a greeting that can be personalized if you can confidently add each contact's first name, such as *Dear Joe* or *Hi Mary*, and of course, end each message with a friendly closing that matches your brand personality, such as *Cheers* or *Best regards*. You can also include a signature block with a real person's name and title to make messages more personal.

Subscription Confirmation Autoresponder

SUBJECT LINE: Details about Your New Subscription

We're delighted that you joined the [insert brand or business name here] community!

As a subscriber, you'll automatically receive updates, useful information, and news about our latest sales and promotions delivered directly to your inbox.

> **Tip**
>
> Note that the text in brackets within the copy samples in this chapter indicate content that you should replace with your own, such as product names and contact information. In addition, underlined text represents anchor text that should be linked to the appropriate web page in the actual email message.

We promise to never spam you or flood your inbox with messages you don't want, and every message will include an unsubscribe link if you ever decide you want to opt out of receiving messages from us in the future (but we hope you don't).

Of course, if you have any questions about your subscription, don't hesitate to contact us at [insert your contact information here].

Purchase Confirmation with Upsell Offer Autoresponder

SUBJECT LINE: Your Order Details and Confirmation

We received your order and are working to get it to you as quickly as possible. Your complete order details are below:

[Insert order details including shipping information]

You May Also Like These Products . . .

Since you like [insert product name included in the customer's order], we thought you might like to peek at these items that customers often purchase together with their [insert product name again but in plural form here].

[Insert pictures, short descriptions, and "view product" buttons that lead to each product's page on your website.]

Watch your email for another message from us confirming when your package goes in the mail, and if you have any questions or concerns about your order, contact our customer service department at [insert contact information] right away.

Shipping Confirmation with Upsell Autoresponder

SUBJECT LINE: Your Package Is on Its Way

Great news! Your package is on its way, so watch your mailbox. You can review all your shipping information below:

[Insert shipping information, including expected arrival date and tracking information if available.]

While you're waiting for your package to arrive, check out these popular products that our customers tell us they love!

[Insert images, descriptions, and "view product" buttons for approximately three of your most popular products that lead to each of those products' pages on your website.]

We appreciate your business and want to make sure you're completely happy, so be sure to contact us at [insert your contact information] if anything isn't perfect with your purchase when it arrives.

SaaS Product Free Trial Expiration Autoresponder

SUBJECT LINE: Your Free Trial of [Insert Product or Service Name] Ends Tomorrow

I'm reaching out to let you know your free trial of [insert product or service name] will expire tomorrow. Make sure you complete the account activation process so you don't loss access to these features and more:

· [Insert useful feature and corresponding benefit.]

· [Insert useful feature and corresponding benefit.]

· [Insert useful feature and corresponding benefit.]

If you have any questions about [insert product or service name], contact me directly at [insert your contact information]. I want to make sure you've gotten the most out of your free trial so you can make the best decision about whether [insert product or service name] is right for you.

Remember, your free trial ends tomorrow. Activate your account now so you can continue using [insert product or service name] without interruption!

Cart Abandonment Autoresponder

SUBJECT LINE: Did You Forget Something?

We noticed you visited [insert website name or URL] but didn't complete your order. We don't want you to miss out! Just click here to return to the site and finish your purchase.

If you're having problems with the site or shopping cart, please contact us at [insert contact information], and we'll help you right away.

Re-engagement One-Time Campaign

SUBJECT LINE: Your Last Email from [insert business or brand name]

You haven't read one of our email messages lately, so we're guessing you don't really want to receive them anymore. While we're sad to see you go, we'll stop sending messages to you.

BUT if we're wrong and you want to continue receiving messages from us, we're thrilled! Just click the big "Keep Sending Me Emails" link below, and we'll continue delivering useful news, updates, and information to your inbox.

<u>Keep Sending Me Emails</u>

If you don't click that big link above, we'll assume you really don't want to hear from us anymore, and we'll take you off our list. Of course, you'll continue to get messages related to any purchases you make, but you won't get informational or promotional messages from us anymore.

Just because we might not be communicating by email anymore doesn't mean we can't stay in touch. Join us on <u>Facebook</u> and <u>Twitter</u> [add any other social media channels that you use here with links as well] where we share all kinds of great content.

PUT WHAT YOU'VE LEARNED INTO ACTION

Strategizing and writing email marketing messages takes time, but the extra thought you put into getting things right makes a significant difference in your results. While email marketing is a marketing tactic that requires continual analysis, testing, and tweaking to maximize your results, you shouldn't feel overwhelmed. Since it's relatively inexpensive compared to other marketing investments, you have room to experiment, learn, and improve. However, you need to dive in and get started first!

This book provides you with a comprehensive foundation so you can build an email marketing program that benefits your brand and business for the long term. Follow the lessons learned, and you'll be on your way to building successful email conversion funnels, brand relationships, and customer loyalty that lead directly to business growth.

Email Marketing Resources

EMAIL MARKETING TOOLS

Learn more in Chapter 4.

- *ActiveCampaign*: www.activecampaign.com
- *AWeber*: http://aweber.com
- *Campaign Monitor*: www.campaignmonitor.com
- *Click Funnels*: www.clickfunnels.com
- *Constant Contact*: www.constantcontact.com
- *ConvertKit*: https://convertkit.com
- *Drip*: www.drip.co
- *Emma*: https://myemma.com
- *GetResponse*: www.getresponse.com
- *iContact*: www.icontact.com
- *Infusionsoft*: www.infusionsoft.com
- *Litmus*: https://litmus.com/
- *Mad Mimi*: https://madmimi.com
- *MailChimp*: https://mailchimp.com
- *Ontraport*: https://ontraport.com
- *SendGrid*: https://sendgrid.com/
- *VerticalResponse*: www.verticalresponse.com

MARKETING AUTOMATION TOOLS

Learn more in Chapter 1.

- *SharpSpring*: https://sharpspring.com
- *Marketo*: www.marketo.com
- *HubSpot*: www.hubspot.com
- *Pardot*: www.pardot.com
- *Infusionsoft*: www.infusionsoft.com
- *Ontraport*: https://ontraport.com
- *ActiveCampaign*: www.activecampaign.com

OPT-IN FORM TOOLS

Learn more in Chapter 6.

- *OptinMonster*: http://optinmonster.com
- *Sumo*: https://sumo.com
- *Unbounce*: https://unbounce.com
- *Leadpages*: www.leadpages.net
- *Instapage*: https://instapage.com
- *MailMunch*: www.mailmunch.co
- *Thrive Themes*: https://thrivethemes.com

LANDING PAGES

Learn more in Chapter 7.

- *Leadpages*: www.leadpages.net/templates
- *Instapage*: https://instapage.com/landing-page-templates
- *Unbounce*: https://unbounce.com/landing-page-templates
- *OptimizePress*: https://marketplace.optimizepress.com

DESIGN TOOLS

Learn more in Chapter 7.

- *Canva*: www.canva.com
- *Stencil*: https://getstencil.com
- *PicMonkey*: www.picmonkey.com
- *Paint.net*: www.getpaint.net
- *Gimp*: www.gimp.org
- *Inkscape*: https://inkscape.org/en

IMAGES, ICONS, AND FONTS

Learn more in Chapter 7.

- *Bigstock*: www.bigstockphoto.com
- *PhotoSpin*: www.photospin.com
- *Creative Market*: https://creativemarket.com
- *IconMonstr*: https://iconmonstr.com
- *MyFonts*: www.myfonts.com

INFOGRAPHIC AND DATA VISUALIZATION TOOLS

Learn more in Chapter 7.

- *Visme*: www.visme.co
- *Piktochart*: https://piktochart.com
- *Venngage*: https://venngage.com
- *Creately*: https://creately.com
- *MindMeister*: www.mindmeister.com

EMAIL DELIVERABILITY

Learn more in Chapter 3.

- *OpenSPF.org*: www.openspf.org
- *SPFWizard.net*: www.spfwizard.net
- *DKIM.org*: www.dkim.org
- *SocketLabs*: www.socketlabs.com/domainkey-dkim-generation-wizard
- *DMARC*: https://dmarc.org/resources/deployment-tools
- *GlobalCyberAlliance*: https://dmarc.globalcyberalliance.org
- *Uribl*: http://uribl.com
- *Surbl*: www.surbl.org
- *Spamhaus*: www.spamhaus.org
- *MultiRBL*: http://multirbl.valli.org

FACEBOOK CONTEST TOOLS

Learn more in Chapter 6.

- *ShortStack*: www.shortstack.com
- *Woobox*: https://woobox.com
- *Wishpond*: www.wishpond.com

VIDEO AND AUDIO TOOLS

Learn more in Chapter 7.

- *Camtasia*: www.techsmith.com/video-editor.html
- *Screencast-O-Matic*: https://screencast-o-matic.com
- *YouTube*: www.youtube.com
- *Vimeo*: https://vimeo.com
- *Dailymotion*: www.dailymotion.com/us
- *Wistia*: https://wistia.com

FILE STORAGE

Learn more in Chapter 7.

- *Dropbox*: www.dropbox.com
- *Google Drive*: https://drive.google.com
- *Box*: www.box.com

ONLINE COURSE PUBLISHING

Learn more in Chapter 8.

- *Teachable*: https://teachable.com
- *Skyprep*: https://skyprep.com
- *DigitalChalk*: www.digitalchalk.com
- *Thinkific*: www.thinkific.com
- *WP Courseware*: https://flyplugins.com/wp-courseware
- *LearnDash*: www.learndash.com
- *LearnPress*: https://wordpress.org/plugins/learnpress
- *Sensei*: https://woocommerce.com/products/sensei

GENERAL FORM TOOLS

Learn more in Chapter 9.

- *Google Forms*: www.google.com/forms/about
- *Formstack*: www.formstack.com
- *JotForm*: www.jotform.com

SURVEY TOOLS

Learn more in Chapter 5.

- *Google Forms*: www.google.com/forms/about
- *SurveyMonkey*: www.surveymonkey.com
- *QuestionPro*: www.questionpro.com

MISCELLANEOUS SOFTWARE AND ONLINE RESOURCES

Learn more in Chapters 3 and 4.

- *Zapier*: https://zapier.com (for software and application integration)
- *Bitly*: https://bitly.com (URL shortener)
- *Google URL Shortener*: https://goo.gl

WEBSITES AND BLOGS

- *Entrepreneur.com*: www.entrepreneur.com
- *Keysplash Creative Inc. Blog*: http://keysplashcreative.com/blog

BOOKS

Kick-ass Copywriting in 10 Easy Steps, Susan Gunelius (Irvine, CA: Entrepreneur Press) 2008.

Ultimate Guide to Facebook Advertising, 3rd Editon, Perry Marshall, Keith Krance, and Thomas Meloche (Irvine, CA: Entrepreneur Press) 2017.

The New Rules of Marketing and PR, 6th Edition, David Meerman Scott (Hoboken, NJ: Wiley) 2017.

DOWNLOADABLE RESOURCES MENTIONED IN CHAPTERS 1 THROUGH 12

Here is a list of URLs for each of the downloadable resources mentioned in this book so far:

Chapter	Resource	Download URL
Chapter 2	Buyer Persona Worksheet	http://ultimateguidetoemailmarketing.com/bpw
Chapter 3	Spam Trigger Words List	http://ultimateguidetoemailmarketing.com/stw
Chapter 10	Subject Line Worksheet	http://ultimateguidetoemailmarketing.com/slw
Chapter 10	Emotional Triggers Power Words Cheat Sheet	http://ultimateguidetoemailmarketing.com/etpw
Chapter 10	Call to Action Cheat Sheet	http://ultimateguidetoemailmarketing.com/cta

Chapter	Resource	Download URL
Chapter 11	Autoresponder Strategy Template	http://ultimateguidetoemailmarketing.com/ast
Chapter 12	Email Marketing Results Worksheet	http://ultimateguidetoemailmarketing.com/emrw
Chapter 13	Swipe File	http://ultimateguidetoemailmarketing.com/sf

Glossary

Authentication: A process that allows internet service providers to verify a message sender's identity using one or more of the three primary authentication methods: Sender Policy Framework (SPF), DomainKeys Identified Mail (DKIM), or Domain-based Message Authentication, Reporting & Conformance (DMARC)

Automated sequence: A series of email messages sent out in a specific order, typically at certain times or after certain actions are completed

Autoresponder: A single email message that is automatically sent in response to a specific action taken

Benefit: What a product or service can do for the customer or how the product or service can help the customer

Blacklist: A list used by internet service providers that identifies an email sender as a spammer

Bounce rate: The percentage of email messages that are not delivered based on hard or soft bounces relative to the number of messages sent

B2B: Marketing and other business efforts targeted to businesses

B2C: Marketing and other business efforts targeted to end user customers

Clickthrough rate: The percentage of clicks an email message receives in relation to the number of people the message was sent to

Content upgrade: Additional content (such as a checklist or worksheet) offered to expand on content a person has already consumed (such as a blog post) with the purpose of obtaining email addresses from prospective customers

Conversion: The completion of a specific, predefined action

Conversion funnel: An automated sequence of email messages created to motivate the recipient to take a specific action, which is identified as a conversion

Copywriting: The use of words in marketing communications to drive an audience to take a business's desired actions

Customer Relationship Management (CRM): Techniques and tools used to manage customers' interactions with a business throughout the customer lifecycle

Deliverability: The ability of a specific email message to successfully arrive in a recipient's inbox

DKIM (DomainKeys Identified Mail): An authentication process used to associate a domain name with an email message, indicating it was created by a known sender (also called a digital signature)

DMARC (Domain Message Authentication Reporting and Conformance): An authentication process used to ensure the sender of an email message is who they claim to be

DNS (Domain Name System) record: A system used to map a URL to an IP address

Email automation: The process of setting up email messages using an email marketing tool so they are sent automatically at predetermined times or when specific actions are completed

Email campaign: An individual email message sent to a list of subscribers (also called an email blast)

Email funnel: A sequence of email messages created to achieve a specific goal when sent in order (e.g., email conversion funnel)

Email sequence: See *automated sequence*

Email service provider (ESP): A company that offers a tool to be used for email marketing, including creating messages, building lists, sending messages, tracking results, and so on

Feature: The parts or characteristics of a product or service

Hard bounce: A permanent failure to deliver a message to an email address, typically because the address does not exist, is invalid, or is blocked

Honeypot: An email address planted into lists and on websites to catch spammers who purchase lists or collect addresses from the internet and send messages to those addresses without permission from the recipients

Internet service provider (ISP): A company that provides users with access to the internet and other services, such as email

IP (Internet Protocol) address: A numerical label assigned to each device connected to a network, which could be unique or shared and is used for identification purposes

Key Performance Indicator (KPI): Metrics used to analyze the success of email marketing messages

Landing page: A web page designed for the sole purpose of persuading visitors to take a specific action (e.g., conversions)

Lead magnet: A piece of content or an offer created to entice people to provide their email addresses in exchange for it

Marketing automation: The process of automating marketing tasks, such as email, social media, sales, and more using a software tool

Marketing funnel: A visual model used to follow consumers through the buyer journey, from lead generation and nurturing to making a purchase

MTA record: Software used to transfer email messages from one computer to another (also called Message Transfer Agent or Mail Transfer Agent)

Open rate: The percentage of recipients who open your email message

Opt-in: Permission given by someone that allows a business to send email messages to that person

SaaS: See *software-as-a-service*

Segment: A subgroup of a larger audience made up of individuals with similar traits

Soft bounce: A temporary failure to deliver a message to an email address, typically because the recipient's inbox is full or the email server is unavailable

Software-as-a-service (SaaS): Online software that users typically pay for through monthly or annual subscriptions

Spam: Email messages sent to recipients that they did not ask for or give permission to be sent

SPF (Sender Policy Framework): An authentication process using a domain name server (DNS) record that says a domain or IP can send email messages on behalf of a specific sender

TXT record: A type of DNS record used by SPF in the authentication process

Unsubscribe: The action taken by contacts on an email marketing list when they opt out of receiving future messages from a business

URL (Uniform Resource Locator): Identifies the specific address of a page on the internet

Whitelist: A list of email addresses or domain names that are excluded from email-blocking programs

About the Author

Susan Gunelius is president and CEO of KeySplash Creative, Inc. (KeySplashCreative.com), a marketing communications company offering copywriting, content marketing, email marketing, social media marketing, and strategic branding services. She spent the first half of her 25-year career directing marketing programs for AT&T and HSBC. Today, her clients include household brands like Citigroup, Cox Communications, Intuit, and more as well as small businesses around the world.

Susan has written 11 marketing-related books that have been translated into multiple languages, including the highly popular *Content Marketing for Dummies, 30-Minute Social Media Marketing*, and *Kick-ass Copywriting in 10 Easy Steps*. She is a recognized marketing and branding expert and writes about these topics for a variety of media publications, including Entrepreneur.com and Forbes.com. Susan also speaks about marketing and branding at events around the world.

She is founder and editor in chief of Women on Business (WomenOnBusiness.com), an award-winning blog for business women, and she is a Certified Career Coach offering personal branding, career strategy, personality assessment, and resume writing services to individuals in a wide variety of careers. She holds a BS in marketing and an MBA in management and strategy.

Susan can be found on social media through Twitter (@susangunelius and @womenonbusiness), Facebook (facebook.com/keysplashcreative and facebook.com/womenonbusiness), and LinkedIn (linkedin.com/in/susangunelius.

Index